Retirement
Breakthrough

Also by Dick Duff

Books

Preserving Family Wealth Using Tax Magic: Strategies Worth Millions

Keep Every Last Dime: How to Avoid 201 Common Estate Planning Traps and Tax Disasters

Money Magic with Annuities: Great Ideas for Creative Investors, 2nd Edition

Take Charge of Your IRA: Avoid Tax Traps and Family Squabbles, 2nd Edition

Optimal Aging: Your Guide from Experts in Medicine, Law, and Finance (Dick Duff is a contributing author)

Reference Manuals

The Annuity Blue Book, 2nd Edition

The IRA Gold Book: Financial Solutions for Clients with Significant IRAs, 2007

Professional Annuity Advisor Essays, 2007

The Basics of Annuity Planning

CD-ROMs

How to Be a Professional Annuity Advisor

The Future of Retirement Income Planning

Audiotape

Taxes, Lawsuits, and Family Conflict (an 8-hour series)

Selected Articles, © 2006–2010

(available at www.ProducersWEB.com)

"My Social Security Program (and Yours)"

"The U.S. Retirement Income System" (a series)

"The Beneficiaries and You"

"Is My Safe Money Safe?" (a series)

"Three Directional Financial Planning" (a series)

"Getting Out of Retirement's Income Mess" (a series)

"An IRA Family Bank"

"Missed Fortune: More Mixed Messages"

"Stretch IRAs: Cutting Edge Planning or an Accident Waiting to Happen?"

Retirement
Breakthrough

The Safe, Secure Way to Guaranteed Income You Can't Outlive—in Any Economy

Dick Duff, JD, CLU

GREENLEAF
BOOK GROUP PRESS

Published by Greenleaf Book Group Press
Austin, Texas
www.gbgpress.com

Distributed by Greenleaf Book Group LLC

For ordering information or special discounts for bulk purchases, please contact Greenleaf Book Group LLC at PO Box 91869, Austin, TX 78709, 512.891.6100.

Design and composition by Greenleaf Book Group LLC
Cover design by Greenleaf Book Group LLC

Publisher's Cataloging-In-Publication Data
(Prepared by The Donohue Group, Inc.)

Duff, Richard W.
    Retirement breakthrough : the safe, secure way to guaranteed income you can't outlive-- in any economy / Dick Duff. -- 1st ed.

    p. ; cm.

    Includes index.
    ISBN: 978-1-60832-025-7

1. Retirement income--Planning. 2. Retirees--Finance, Personal. 3. Retirement--Planning. 4. Saving and investment. I. Title.

HG179 .D84 2010
332.024/014   2010920229

Part of the Tree Neutral™ program, which offsets the number of trees consumed in the production and printing of this book by taking proactive steps, such as planting trees in direct proportion to the number of trees used: www.treeneutral.com

TreeNeutral

Printed in the United States of America on acid-free paper

10 11 12 13 14 10 9 8 7 6 5 4 3 2 1

First Edition

*To my son, Scott, his wife, Katherine,
and their children, Jared and Tori*

DISCLAIMER

I wrote *Retirement Breakthrough* to inform readers about high-level planning strategies that are rarely covered in consumer magazines or the financial advice columns in newspapers. These strategies—and the underlying concepts—are not always easy to grasp. In an effort to make them clear, I have used many *hypothetical* examples throughout the book.

Let me stress the word "hypothetical." Please understand that you may not be able to duplicate the features of every single example—exactly as described—in the real world. For instance, I may say a savings vehicle is capable of generating 5 percent compounded interest annually—a number I have chosen to make the math simpler to follow—but you may find, upon investigation, that the savings vehicle offers a different rate.

These examples are meant to be general in nature. It is my purpose to educate you—not to give you specific legal or tax advice. For that, you will need to consult your attorney; accountant; or other members of your financial, tax, and estate planning team. Only individuals who know your specific facts and circumstances—and the specific laws in your state—can give you responsible, appropriate advice. Realize, too, that state and federal laws do change, so always consult your attorney to make sure that the law—as expressed here—is correct before making any decisions.

CONTENTS

FOREWORD

Individuals suffering through the new financial sobriety wonder if anything will ever be the same again. As reality tests the economic fiber of the country, some of us are looking skyward to see if Old Glory is still flying. I'm glad to report she is still waving high and mighty, but what about your personal economic flag? Is *it* still flying high, or did you strike your flag in that old gesture of surrender to the enemy?

From where I sit, as vice president of Presidential Life Insurance Company, it seems to me that there are as many people who diligently set aside money for retirement only to suffer seemingly irreversible financial loss as there are those who want a good retirement but don't even know where to begin. That's what makes *Retirement Breakthrough: The Safe, Secure Way to Guaranteed Income You Can't Outlive . . . in any Economy* so timely. My longtime friend, Dick Duff, an icon in the insurance industry, speaks to people in both situations. In this book, his newest, he provides the same kind of guidance a good coach would when his team is far behind.

When that happens, a good coach will drag the players back through the basic drills. In sports, those include "blocking and tackling" in football, "hitting and catching" in baseball, and "picking and rolling" in basketball. In personal finance, the basics include generating savings, making smart use of annuities and life insurance, establishing Individual Retirement Accounts (IRAs), and buying your own home. Dick will take you through all these drills. He'll help you understand—probably in a way you never have before—why each of these is so important.

He'll also show you how to execute a good "defense"—in this case, asset protection planning strategies that can help you hold on to the money you *do* have, especially when someone else has designs on your money. In litigious times like these and with so many bankruptcy filings, asset protection planning is essential.

—

You may not have heard of Dick before, but in my industry, he's very well known. His books line the shelves of many financial advisors, and his columns are well read. Over the years, his financial sagacity has caused him to be a heavily sought-after writer and lecturer.

For as long as I have known him, Dick has delivered the same consistent message: Financial success is built on a solid foundation and won over the long haul. In this book, he explains how to create that no-fail foundation. He takes a conservative, balanced, and thoughtful approach.

If you have been lucky enough to avoid economic hardship in these times, but you still have a nagging feeling of vulnerability—as if you might be next—this book will reassure you. What Dick offers is time tested, and it works. Annuity contracts, for example, hark back to the days of the early Roman Empire. In the Greco-Roman era, the average life expectancy was 36 years for a woman and 42 to 43 years for a man. Today, when life expectancy is so much longer, annuities are even more necessary to hedge against outliving your money.

If you are age 65 or older, I recommend that you pay particular attention to the chapters on life insurance and annuity contracts. You might not have thought about these financial instruments when the market was doing well, but you'd be smart to do so now. Life insurance is one way to make up for estate losses, and annuity contracts are powerful income-generating machines. These financial products can work to replace lost assets and income.

If you are young, ages 25 to 35, and heavily in debt—perhaps from a home purchase and college loans that are not yet paid off—take a deep breath. Study the charts in the first chapter and learn how money multiplies over time. Determine how much you'll need to retire comfortably. Both will motivate you to save as much as you can, for as long as you can. (The old saying "cash is king" has never been more true.) If all you can do for now is put loose coins in a jar, do it! The chapters on IRAs and home ownership will be helpful too.

If you're in that middle group, ages 35 to 60, you may be feeling the most stressed. So many in this age group have suffered financial loss via their retirement plans, personal residence devaluations, and perhaps job loss—even as they struggle to pay for the cost of college education for their kids and elder care for their parents. This may be the time to establish, or reestablish, a solid financial foundation.

Now that much of the excess and exuberance is out of the system, the realization is starting to take hold that it is up to individuals to control their financial destiny. The more engaged you are in your own financial affairs, the more control you retain and the less power you cede to individuals and institutions that may not have your best interests at heart.

Retirement Breakthrough can give you the understanding you need to do so. It will help you fully comprehend the ramifications of your own personal financial decisions and the financial products you purchase. Understanding breeds confidence, confidence builds winners, and winners win championships!

So if you want to win—if you want a long-term successful financial outcome—pay heed to the advice in the pages ahead.

The message is clear: You can do it, it takes time, and you will get there.

Gary S. Mettler, CFP, CEBS
Vice President
Presidential Life Insurance Company
Nyack, NY

INTRODUCTION

---

*I am more concerned about the return of my money
than the return on my money.*
—Mark Twain

---

*"Safe and secure . . . Need to get back to the basics! . . . Who can I
trust? . . . Can't go through these losses again . . . "*

As an online columnist with a long career in the insurance business, I am acutely aware of the importance of financial security in people's lives.

With time comes a little wisdom, they say. During my 45 years of working with people on their estate and financial planning, I've seen my clients—or my clients' clients—through their ups and downs: divorces, health issues, losses in the market, and the "such a deal I've got for you schemes"—not once or twice, but for some, two, three, and four times in their lives. My experiences have led me to write a number of books: *Preserving Family Wealth, Keep Every Last Dime, Take Charge of Your IRA,* and *Money Magic with Annuities.*

In *Retirement Breakthrough,* the message is one of hope. Yes, even in economically troubled times, it *is* possible to create a financially secure retirement. But you have to be willing to get back to the basics, while also using proven financial strategies relevant for today's market and the laws, rules, and regulations that apply. A plan that harks back to the basics is, in my mind, the *only* way to get there. And by "there," I mean having enough income to live worry free so you can use all of your energy to pursue hobbies, enjoy your grandchildren, travel with loved ones, and give time to causes you feel strongly about. Or you might find part-time work in a field that interests you—something you *really* enjoy, for a change. Planning ahead so that you can live that kind of life in retirement can bring great satisfaction.

—

I've been fortunate to grow up seeing life from a conservative vantage point. I was an Iowa farm boy. In fact, I grew up on a farm in Madison County, Iowa. When you grow up on a farm, you get up early and go to bed late. Most days are the same. You learn to work hard and find that if you do, things will usually turn out okay. The dominant philosophy in my community was agrarian, bound by a Puritan work ethic. In short, the belief was that virtue resides in the land and hard work is a form of personal salvation.

What does this have to do with retirement income planning? A lot! That lifestyle taught discipline. And discipline is the right approach to working with capital over a long period of time. A slow, steady, and consistent income-building plan for retirement income makes sense. Once this kind of foundation is in place, you can explore opportunities that require greater tolerance for risk.

Of course, not all people have patience for a safe and steady approach. That's when they are vulnerable to financial and other kinds of loss. I've seen clients and friends chase the Brass Ring and lose their balance. Instead of mastering money, they allowed it to control them. This can have grave consequences. A few aggressive business people I knew died far too young, including two who committed suicide when finances went sour.

I also have seen those who live in fear of dying broke. They don't seek out good advisors (partly because they're tight-fisted), and yet they miss out on valuable financial guidance. So they never learn about the kinds of special strategies that could solve their money worries and give them peace of mind. What a waste. They also turn money—or the fear of not having enough—into a master when it should be a servant. And those without any plan take helter-skelter jobs just to keep food on the table. They may even live in fear of becoming wards in a nursing home—not of their choice.

People who have a solid core retirement income plan are different. They *are* the masters of their money: they plan ahead so they have the means to enjoy themselves and decide how they will use their time. But life isn't always fair, even to those smart enough to plan for their financial future. I've heard from plenty of people who are frantic to keep assets that are threatened by lawsuits, bankruptcies, and foreclosures. They don't want to lose what they've worked for, but, frequently, they do. That's because they haven't taken advantage of asset protection planning, a philosophy and set of strategies I will teach you so you can protect your hard earned money from others who want it.

I stress safety. In my book, saving money safely comes first. (I'm not much on risky investments.) When you save, you don't gamble your capital (or principal). You simply build on it. Market risk and luck aren't involved. And yes, realize that this wasn't mainstream thinking (at least with day traders and speculators) before the 50 percent market meltdowns, 401(k) losses, and home mortgage disasters.

Today, most people can see value in safe and secure money solutions. They'll go to the Internet for ideas. They welcome a good advisor, if one can be found. If this is what you want, *Retirement Breakthrough* is the right book for you. It will show you how to combine safety with special planning strategies that make optimal use of current financial thinking. These are the keys. You'll make the system work for you, not against you. You and your advisor will create and then implement the optimal retirement income plan for you. It could look stodgy, but it will explode around the edges.

Retirement Breakthrough is not about getting rich quick. I come to this as an educator, rather than as a planner with products to sell. Let me show you what works—and why—so you can tailor your retirement income planning to your individual circumstances. These are time-tested strategies you can count on.

A BLUEPRINT FOR A SAFE, SECURE WAY TO GUARANTEED INCOME YOU CAN'T OUTLIVE

Retirement Breakthrough is the first book ever on retirement income that aims to translate advanced planning concepts usually reserved for expert planners into consumer-friendly language. Its goal: to give you a *blueprint for financial security*. This blueprint will take you from where you are today to where you need to go. With *commitment, discipline,* and *continual review with a financial planner,* you can reach your core retirement goals in a conservative, predictable, and stress-free way. You can eliminate the disasters, the gut wrenching worries, the sleepless nights, and the embarrassment of having failed.

Admittedly, my emphasis on financial security is *not* sexy! Nor is it complicated. It does not take an MBA degree from Harvard to understand, although some regard for simple math will help. This blueprint just requires the discipline to save regularly in quality, proven financial instruments that meet five tests:

1. The instrument needs to be capable of delivering a safe and sustainable return, say 5 percent on average.

2. The instrument needs to offer tax advantages (because a safe 5 percent return can become more like 7 or 8 percent if growth builds tax free, or with a tax deduction).

3. The instrument should provide protection from bankruptcies, lawsuits, and financial threats to you and your family.

4. The instrument should be capable of delivering a guaranteed lifelong income in retirement that comes on time, every time, anywhere in the world.

5. The instrument must help you feel so secure that you won't withdraw and spend your money—or succumb to tempting get-rich-quick schemes and short-term solutions that amount to financial sabotage.

Following through on this blueprint for financial security is like building a dream house. The first four "requirements" are bricks and mortar. They give the foundation its strength. The fifth comes out of the first four. When you commit to a shrewd retirement income plan that is tax-advantaged and protected from claimants, you'll be less likely to switch to something risky, or cash out early. You will be less vulnerable to the Bernie Madoffs of this world, who promise extraordinary returns.

Once a foundation is in place, then you can include market risk and all the extras (the financial equivalent of, say, an extra wing, a pool, or a palatial entrance)—whatever it is that your heart desires. After all, this is *your* plan. You can add anything, as long as you set it on a strong and stable foundation.

Retirement Breakthrough will show you how to build that foundation step by step. In the first part, I will explain how to determine the retirement income "capital" you need to maintain your lifestyle year after year, after adjusting the amount for inflation, amortization of your capital, social security income, and the like. I'll provide handy tables and formulas that show how money builds over time. Then we'll look at how to make optimal use of tax law and asset protection law. These first three chapters will "condition" your thinking for success and help keep your financial planners on their toes.

In the next part of the book, I'll cover in detail four savings instruments you can use—in combination—to create the solid foundation for your retirement income plan. They are:

1. Life insurance values, which offer tax-deferred growth (and other tax advantages), creditor protection, and the potential for guaranteed lifetime income;

2. Annuity values, which offer tax-deferred growth (and other tax advantages), creditor-protection, and the assurance of a guaranteed lifetime income;

3. IRAs (and 401(k)s and company pensions), which can give tax deductions, tax deferral, creditor protection, and tax-free incomes (in the case of a Roth IRA); and

4. A personal residence, which can give tax deductions, tax-free appreciation, creditor protection, and provide an indirect source of guaranteed lifetime income.

Due to such compelling financial features (and the good chance of getting a steady, sustainable rate of return in the first two), people who park their money in these savings instruments tend to leave them intact, only withdrawing money as a last resort.

Of course, none of these four vehicles on their own can perfectly meet my five tests. Taken together, however, they come close. That is why this book covers all four, rather than focusing on, say, a single strategy, as many retirement income books do. I will show you how to use these savings vehicles in combination to make the most of your money.

Then in chapter 10, I'll explain the most efficient ways to pass along whatever's left—whether through your will or beneficiary designation forms.

WHAT YOU CAN DO WITH A LITTLE FINANCIAL INGENUITY

Here's a taste of how far you can go with a little financial ingenuity. In the chapters in the second part of this book, I'll introduce you to many strategies like this one. In Part 1, we'll cover the underpinnings on which these strategies rest.

This example comes straight from real life. A 71-year-old friend told me she was about to inherit $250,000. "I want to make the most of it," she said. "I am thinking of putting it into a five-year CD, but the returns are miserably low. Can you help me do better?"

She told me she wanted to leave a nice amount to her son when she died.

I did some quick calculations. I told her the CD (certificate of deposit) would pay her $6,250 annually for five years, a mere 2½ percent.

"Don't put it in a CD," I advised. "It has three strikes against it. "The return is too low, the income would be fully taxable, and in the event of an unforeseen lawsuit, it could be seized by a creditor."

"What should I do then?"

I suggested the following:

1. Spend $67,000 of that sum on a $250,000 life insurance policy guaranteed to pay $250,000, as long as you die before age 100. This will give your son the entire $250,000 sum when you die.

2. Spend another $68,000 on a single premium immediate annuity, which would guarantee you a *life-long* annual income of $6,250. Most of that income would be tax free, so you'd keep more of your money than if you had invested in a CD. That would leave you with $115,000 to do with as you pleased. You could use it yourself or invest a little more in improvements or variations on the life insurance and annuity for an even better yield.

How's that for maximizing the value of $250,000? My friend reduces her tax bite, provides herself with a life-long income stream, provides the entire $250,000 as an eventual life insurance payment to her son—and has $115,000 to spare!

That's just a quick illustration of how you can improve your financial results when you know your way around the alternative savings vehicles I cover in this book. Ask your financial advisor for more information.

WHO THIS BOOK IS FOR

I wrote *Retirement Breakthrough* for people who want to get smarter about money. It's for those who want a quality life for 30 to 40 years in retirement and are willing to take the responsibility now to make sure they have enough money to do so. This book is just as useful for the healthy retiree with several good decades ahead as it is for the pre-retiree just beginning to plan.

Retirement Breakthrough translates sophisticated planning concepts into language a general reader can understand, which is a boon for financial advisors, too. If you are a general reader, the information in this book can raise the level of the conversation with your financial planner(s). The knowledge you gain will put you in control of your retirement income and give you ideas for planning concepts that may only be familiar to lawyers, accountants, and financial planners. If you are a planner, it can assist you with client education. You can use this book to introduce planning concepts to your clients and get them enthusiastic about your recommendations.

HOW TO USE THIS BOOK

If you want to understand the thinking behind my retirement income blueprint, start at the beginning of the book and read on through. The first three chapters help you become smart about retirement income planning in a broad sense, which will inform your thinking when you have choices to make.

If you have an immediate interest in one of the four financial instruments covered in this book, or in beneficiary planning, you may want to begin with that chapter. At some point later, however, do come back and read the first three chapters. "How Much Money Will I Need in Retirement?" will help you determine your retirement accumulation goal, the starting point for all planning. "From Taxable into Tax free" will train you on the tax implications of any strategy; obviously, the less paid in taxes—legally—the more you keep. And "Protecting Your Savings from Claimants" will explain how to put protective plans in place long before you need them, so that you need never fear losing everything to an unexpected lawsuit—even a bankruptcy.

Once you get into Part 2 on life insurance values, annuity values, individual retirement accounts/qualified plans, and ownership of a personal residence, you'll find relevant background information and both simple *and* advanced action strategies. You will also find greater detail on the asset protection features of each savings vehicle, which will help you preserve what you've worked so hard to build.

Reading and acting on this information will energize you. You'll implement strategies that put concerns behind you, and you will worry less. Worrying, as you probably know, gets you more of what you don't want. Thinking—in the right way—moves you closer to your goals.

My sincere hope is that *Retirement Breakthrough* helps you think productively rather than worry, sleep better at night, take the steps you need, and fully enjoy some super years in your retirement.

A Personal Note

Powerful stuff, isn't it? I am convinced you will like the planning concepts inside. To give you even more understanding of how to apply them to your situation, go to www.retirementbreakthrough-NOW.com. You'll find fascinating and innovative services that will help you build your rock-solid retirement income plan.

Part I

INCREASE YOUR "MONEY INTELLIGENCE"

HOW MUCH MONEY WILL I NEED IN RETIREMENT?

I've got all the money I need
if I die by four o'clock this afternoon.
—*Henry "Henny" Youngman*

According to the 19th Annual Retirement Confidence Survey (RCS), released in the spring of 2009, a record-low 13 percent of the individuals surveyed said they were "very confident" of "having enough money to live comfortably in retirement." That means 87 percent were less than very confident. That's understandable, based on the fact that some of you—baby boomers, typically, according to polls—have been less than diligent about putting money aside for retirement, others have sustained the loss of pension and other retirement benefits due to employer cutbacks (or stinginess), and still others (myself included) have taken a hit when the market tumbled. Because I believe in taking the safe approach, however, I made sure to plan for—and generate—a large enough financial base that was secure from most risk. That is what has allowed me to sleep at night. In the pages ahead, I will show you how to do the same.

That said, I am not insensitive to the kinds of losses many individuals have sustained as the market soured, or mistakes they've made because they lack information about specific financial instruments. I know that some retirees have had to return to work, and others have sweat bullets when they've read their investment statements and realized the magnitude of their losses in the market. Here are some very real scenarios of the ways individuals and families have suffered—needlessly—during these tough financial times. I say "needlessly" because each could have used the concepts in this book to make their losses less severe. As I said, I stress safety throughout the book—and I hope you pick up on this theme, too, and insist on safety first as you put together your own retirement income plan. Realize, too, that there are "safe" ways to recover lost income—I will share those strategies later on. Don't let the sting of a large loss cause you to take a foolish risk in the name of a "quick" recovery.

Here is that list of "avoidable disasters." *Retirement Breakthrough* will give you the know-how to steer clear of each and every one of them. The information in the book will put you in control so that you don't become a victim of circumstance.

1. Stock market meltdown

Georgia lost 50 percent of her retirement income capital in a stock market meltdown. (She also lost one-half of her income in retirement—or so she thought.) Fortunately, a friend referred her to an astute financial advisor, who helped her get over her anger and stress about the losses, so that she could make clearer decisions. He showed Georgia how to restore her income fully with annuities—something I will outline for you later in this book, especially in chapter 7. Of course, an advisor can help you tailor your plan so that it best suits your own facts and circumstances.

2. Missed distributions from an IRA

Paul, a happily married man with children, grandchildren, and lots of enjoyable hobbies, leads a full life. Little wonder he didn't take the time to pay close attention to his IRA accounts—or the rules that apply to them. So when he turned age 70, he missed taking required distributions from his IRA. This went on for several years—and the costs kept adding up. He owed income taxes, a 50 percent penalty tax, and back interest—a real bummer. (In chapter 8, "IRAs and QPs: Basic and Advanced Strategies," I go over the rules so you won't trip over them like this.)

3. Unexpected taxable income in a life insurance policy

Harry had a $500,000 cash value insurance policy. Over his retirement years, he borrowed $200,000 from the contract. This amount was equal to the $200,000 in premiums he had paid in. So when he cancelled the policy (and there was no money), there was no profit and no income tax. Right?

Wrong! Harry's insurance company told him he had $100,000 in taxable income. These were interest expenses he hadn't paid on the policy loans. If he had only kept the policy until his death, the proceeds would have been tax free. (Chapters 4 and 5 cover the ins and outs of borrowing from your cash value life insurance contract.)

4. When an inheritance really mattered

John and Dorothy purchased annuities and cash value life insurance, beefed up their IRAs and 401(k)s, and paid down their mortgage. Their goals: more tax stability and income, asset protection, and probate avoidance.

When John died, most of his assets passed under beneficiary forms instead of wills prepared by his lawyer. There were extra taxes and some members of his family were cut out. His disgruntled heirs sued his advisors.

Everyone meant well, but—without full understanding of the best way to bequeath assets to heirs—mistakes were made and the results were awful. (You can avoid these mistakes if you take to heart the strategies I outline in chapter 10, "Something for Beneficiaries Too.")

5. A good estate plan turned bad

George sold some valuable stock. Judy, his advisor, helped him gift the proceeds into life insurance policies for family. George died 3 years later, and his family became wealthy from the insurance. Sadly, in the meantime, the old stock went up considerably. Lawyers claimed lost profits and interest on the stock that was sold. They wanted it all. I was an expert witness in this case. The judge didn't understand what had been done. The case was settled, and Judy lost. Greed was rampant here. In retrospect, Judy should have involved George's heirs in the planning. I hope there is better communication about money in your family.

6. A commonly poor asset protection plan

Tom chose to put his money into CDs, treasuries, mutual funds, and even gold. He was pleased with the overall package. Later, his home went into foreclosure. His attorney told him that he faced bankruptcy since his investments didn't add up to what he owed. Had he put his savings in annuities and cash value life insurance— as I recommend throughout the book—Tom's savings would have been fully protected from his claimants under the laws in his state.

7. An IRA rollover that wasn't a rollover

Bob and Cheryl inherited their father's 401(k) account and promptly took out the money. Then they "rolled over" their distribution to an IRA in their names.

Soon Bob and Cheryl learned that they owed about $100,000 in income taxes on their distribution. There really wasn't a rollover—at least not one that was tax free. Almost any advisor could have helped and told them what to do. Unfortunately, they went at this alone. (In chapter 8, "IRAs and QPs: Basic and Advanced Strategies," I carefully explain the essentials of this complex subject. However, I caution you to get expert help whenever you attempt a rollover.)

I don't mean to scare you, but as these scenarios suggest, the most well-meaning efforts to create a solid retirement income plan—or a plan to bequeath your assets—can go awry when you are not properly informed about all of the details you need. If you read the book carefully from cover to cover, this shouldn't be a problem for you. The information in the pages ahead will give you the means to "break through" to a whole new level of prosperity in your golden years.

HOW MUCH WILL YOUR DESIRED LIFESTYLE COST?

That's up to you. What lifestyle do you desire? Do you know how much capital you'll need to achieve it? If not, let me show you how to arrive at a figure that accounts for taxes, inflation, Social Security, and the likely rate at which your retirement savings will grow and be spent in retirement. Your personal income plan must embrace all of these variables—and then some.

This is an excellent way to start your retirement income plan—because you will end up with a goal you can work toward. Let's start with a six-step exercise that will help you understand how these variables affect the amount you'll need. Don't worry if the calculations seem daunting. Just try your best and jot down what you come up with. This exercise will also help you see what you know—and what you need to learn—to calculate a retirement income goal.

To keep things as simple as possible, I am going to ask you to imagine you are a 40-year-old with an annual income of $50,000. Imagine, further, that you are willing to make a healthy $10,000 annual contribution for the next 25 years—until you are age 65—to a savings vehicle that earns a steady 5 percent interest. (I am choosing to use a 5 percent interest rate here—and will do so throughout the book—partly for convenience's sake, because it simplifies the math. It also seems like a reasonable, conservative rate of return that can be achieved long term, on average. That said, however, keep in mind that 5 percent is just an "assumption," and not a *given*, since interest rates fluctuate over time.)

Let's also assume that you want to maintain the same standard of living in retirement that you currently enjoy, and you don't want to run out of money. Will your savings plan accomplish your goal? To find out, use the following steps:

1. Estimate how much money you'll accumulate 25 years from now. Don't use a calculator. Make a good guess.

2. Determine how much capital you'll *actually* need (Steps 2–6). Calculate 80 percent of your present spendable income as an "income in retirement" goal. Your spendable income here is $40,000–$50,000, less savings of $10,000. Eighty percent of that $40,000—$32,000—is your retirement income goal. Now determine the retirement income capital at age 65—the sum at 5 percent interest that will pay you $32,000 annually. (Hint: Try $640,000! $640,000 × .05 = $32,000.)

3. Increase your income goal by an inflation rate compounded annually—for each year between your present age and age 65. For convenience, I'll choose a 3½ percent inflation rate, which should double your income requirement to $64,000 somewhere between ages 60 and 65. Then adjust your retirement income capital goal by doubling it as well. That brings

the retirement income capital goal to $1,280,000 (2 × $640,000).

4. Increase your income goal from Step 2 once again, to plan for inflation at 3½ percent *after* retirement. (This will nearly double your income after, say, another 20 years at age 85.) Look at it this way: You'll need to increase your retirement income capital, as determined in Step 3, by about 50 percent to reflect a median income in retirement between age 66 and 85. (Hint: That median income is $89,000.)

5. Amortize your retirement income capital as determined in Step 4 over 20 years in retirement. (*Amortizing* refers to the process of "spending down" a retirement kitty, where the remaining capital continues to earn interest.) Naturally, you'll need less capital because it is being spent down to zero and not kept intact.

6. Reduce your retirement income capital goal (Step 5) to account for income from Social Security. What's the difference? That's the actual retirement income capital you'll need.

Well, how did you do? How does your savings goal in Step 1 compare with the amount you'll actually need from Step 6? If there is a shortfall, what adjustments can you make to fill in the gap? If you cannot answer these questions now, you *will* be able to at the end of the chapter, after I show you how to do the calculations. You might just amaze yourself.

IF MATH ISN'T YOUR THING . . .

You can come back to this chapter later. This chapter and the next— on how to reduce your tax bite—are more math intensive than any other chapter in the book, so don't judge the difficulty of this book by these two chapters. That said, I am confident that you can grasp the math in these two chapters. I've done my best to simplify it.

The math exercises in this chapter will help you calculate an income for your personal retirement plan and show you how numbers relate over time. Once you understand present and future values, compound interest, and the Rule of 72, you will be able to arrive rather quickly at how much money you'll need in retirement.

If you choose to skip over this chapter and/or the next, *do* come back to them. Please don't be intimidated; I mean what I say about *simple* math. If you still don't want to do the calculations, at least skim things so you can become familiar with the basic concepts. Doing so will give you a better grasp of the chapters on specific financial savings vehicles.

PRESENT AND FUTURE VALUES, COMPOUND INTEREST, AND THE RULE OF 72

Before I explain how to do the actual calculations to arrive at your retirement income capital goal, I'd like to prepare you with a series of simple, finance-related math exercises that will help you think about numbers in a very interesting way. My hope is that these will inform your thinking throughout the book and discussions with your own financial planners. It will also help make Steps 1 through 6 that much easier.

In this section, we'll look at present and future values (PVs and FVs), compound interest, and the Rule of 72. For those of you who aren't familiar with these, they are fascinating—and extremely useful—financial planning tools. In practical terms, your money always has present values (now) that could be on their way to future values (later), depending on what you do with it.

I learned about these early on. In fact, I've been interested in how numbers relate to each other for as long as I can remember. As a child, I used to multiply and divide numbers on auto license plates and work with sports statistics. Algebra formulas and calculus didn't interest me. Instead, I liked my math plain and simple. For me, it was about whether a column of numbers looked right or didn't.

The problems I will take you through will help you develop the same sense. Although there are a lot of numbers and calculations in this chapter, you don't have to be a math genius to get through these— I promise. To make things easier, I am mostly rounding everything to the nearest hundred or thousand. Have fun with these.

Let's begin by looking at how money grows over time, aided by different interest rates. (Again, we'll assume a "safe" rate of 5 percent and occasionally a more "aggressive" rate of 8 percent.)

Ready to begin? Then please take a close look at Chart 1, "The Results of Various Rates of Return on One Dollar of Principal Paid at the Beginning of Year One" on page 23. Chart 1 is loaded with helpful information. Use it to solve Problems 1 through 8.

Problem 1: Setting aside a sum safely at 5 percent

Let's assume that you are in your early to mid-40s, and you receive a gift, inheritance, bonus, or lottery prize of $100,000. You want a safe investment—one that's fairly certain to pay 5 percent interest (on average), so you choose certificates of deposit (CDs), treasuries, and bonds. What can you expect to have on hand in 10 years? Or in 20 years, if you retire in your mid-60s?

You'll find the answers in Chart 1. Go to the "5%" column on the top line and scroll down to the 10th year. Since $1 building at 5 percent compound interest over 10 years will grow to $1.63 (actually $1.629), 100,000 one-dollar bills will grow to $162,900. In 20 years, when you are in your early 60s, you'll have $265,300. See, that's not too hard, is it?

Note: When it comes to PVs and FVs in this example, $100,000 earning 5 percent (over 10 years) is the *present value* of $162,900, and $162,900 is the *future value* of $100,000 earning 5 percent over a 10-year period.

Problem 2: Another way to look at money growing

We just saw that $100,000 at 5 percent interest will grow to $162,900 in 10 years. Is there another way to calculate what you'll have in 20 years? Yes! Just multiply $162,900 by $1.629. (That works out to the same: $265,300.) You don't even need the Chart 1 numbers at the 20th year. To get the result for each succeeding 10-year period, keep multiplying by 1.629.

Problem 3: Saving for a specific goal

Consider the flip side: building a sum of money to a specific goal. Say the goal is $265,300 in 20 years. To determine how much to set aside (assuming a 5 percent earnings rate), divide $265,300 by 2.653 (which you'll find under the 5% column at the 20th year). You'll get $100,000. That's the lump sum to save or invest.

Note: Chart 1 is helpful for both the "contributions" and "benefits" perspective on growing a retirement kitty. Multiply a lump sum (a contribution) by the numerical factors to reach a lump sum or benefit. Alternately, divide a goal or target (a benefit) by the appropriate factor to obtain a single input or contribution.

Problem 4: Setting aside a sum aggressively at 8 percent

A financial planner proposes to invest money at about 8 percent annually. If you look at Chart 1 under the 20th year in the 8% column, you'll see that you could possibly accumulate $466,100

Chart 1

The Results of Various Rates of Return on One Dollar of Principal Paid at the Beginning of Year One

					Rate				
Year	3%	4%	5%	6%	7%	8%	9%	10%	12%
1	$1.030	$1.040	$1.050	$1.060	$1.070	$1.080	$1.090	$1.100	$1.120
2	1.060	1.082	1.102	1.124	1.145	1.166	1.188	1.210	1.254
3	1.093	1.125	1.158	1.191	1.225	1.260	1.295	1.331	1.405
4	1.126	1.170	1.216	1.262	1.311	1.360	1.412	1.464	1.574
5	1.159	1.217	1.276	1.338	1.403	1.469	1.539	1.611	1.762
6	1.194	1.265	1.340	1.419	1.501	1.587	1.677	1.772	1.974
7	1.230	1.316	1.407	1.504	1.606	1.714	1.828	1.949	2.211
8	1.267	1.369	1.477	1.594	1.718	1.851	1.993	2.144	2.476
9	1.305	1.423	1.551	1.689	1.838	1.999	2.172	2.358	2.773
10	1.344	1.480	1.629	1.791	1.967	2.159	2.367	2.594	3.106
11	1.384	1.539	1.710	1.898	2.105	2.332	2.580	2.853	3.479
12	1.426	1.601	1.796	2.012	2.252	2.518	2.813	3.138	3.896
13	1.489	1.665	7.886	2.133	2.410	2.720	3.066	3.452	4.363
14	1.513	1.732	1.980	2.261	2.579	2.937	3.342	3.797	4.887
15	1.558	1.801	2.079	2.397	2.759	3.172	3.642	4.177	5.474
16	1.605	1.873	2.183	2.540	2.952	3.426	3.970	4.595	6.130
17	1.653	1.948	2.292	2.693	3.159	3.700	4.238	5.054	6.866
18	1.702	2.026	2.407	2.854	3.380	3.996	4.717	5.560	7.690
19	1.754	2.107	2.527	3.026	3.617	4.316	5.142	6.116	8.613
20	1.806	2.191	2.653	3.207	3.870	4.661	5.604	6.727	9.646
21	1.860	2.279	2.786	3.400	4.141	5.034	6.109	7.400	10.804
22	1.916	2.370	2.925	3.604	4.430	5.437	6.659	8.140	12.100
23	1.974	2.465	3.072	3.820	4.741	5.871	7.258	8.954	13.552
24	2.033	2.563	3.225	4.049	5.072	6.341	7.911	9.850	15.179
25	2.094	2.666	3.386	4.292	5.427	5.848	8.623	10.835	17.000
26	2.157	2.772	3.556	4.549	5.807	7.396	9.399	11.918	19.040
27	2.221	2.883	3.733	4.822	6.214	7.988	10.245	13.110	21.325
28	2.288	2.979	3.920	5.112	6.649	8.627	11.167	14.421	23.884
29	2.357	3.119	4.116	5.418	7.114	9.317	12.172	15.863	26.750
30	2.428	3.243	4.322	5.743	7.612	10.163	13.268	17.449	29.960
31	2.500	3.373	4.538	6.088	8.145	10.868	14.462	19.194	33.555
32	2.575	3.508	4.765	6.453	8.715	11.737	15.763	21.114	37.582
33	2.652	3.648	5.003	6.841	9.325	12.676	17.182	23.225	42.092
34	2.732	3.794	5.253	7.251	9.978	13.690	18.728	25.548	47.143
35	2.814	3.946	5.516	7.686	10.677	14.785	20.414	28.102	52.800

($100,000 × 4.661) if the financial planner is right. In other words, a mere 3 percent greater return builds a cool extra $200,800 ($466,100 less $265,300) over a 20-year period.

There are always two paths to an income in retirement. One is safe and secure. The other is less certain, but may require less to set aside. This book emphasizes a safe and secure approach, where I assume that roughly 5 percent interest is attainable, on average, over a long period of time. However, you'll always have choices.

Now for my all-time favorite—the Rule of 72! Here's the deal.

Problem 5: The fascinating Rule of 72—how money doubles over time

Again, you have that $100,000 and want to double this sum some day. How long will that take?

It depends. If you know the rate of earnings, simply divide that into 72 to determine the number of years to conclusion. (Or, if you know the years, divide them into 72 and learn the rate you must earn.) That's the incredibly handy Rule of 72. Here are some examples:

$100,000 at 3% will double in 24 (72 ÷ 3) years.
$100,000 at 4% will double in 18 (72 ÷ 4) years.
$100,000 at 5% will double in 14 (72 ÷ 5) years.
$100,000 at 6% will double in 12 (72 ÷ 6) years.
$100,000 at 7% will double in 10 (72 ÷ 7) years
$100,000 at 8% will double in 9 (72 ÷ 8) years.
$100,000 at 9% will double in 8 (72 ÷ 9) years.
$100,000 at 10% will double in 7 (72 ÷ 10) years.
$100,000 at 12% will double in 6 (72 ÷ 12) years.

I know it doesn't seem possible, but it is! To prove it to yourself, go to Chart 1 and compare the factors in **bold** in the next paragraph to these Rule of 72 examples.

Start with the 3% column, and then go down to Year 24 in that column. You will see that $1 earning 3 percent interest becomes **$2.03** after 24 years. At 4 percent interest, that same dollar will become **$2.03** after just 18 years. A dollar earning 5 percent interest gets you **$1.98** in 14 years; while 6 percent interest gets **$2.01** in 12 years; 7 percent, **$1.97** in 10 years; 8 percent, **$2.00** in 9 years; 9 percent, **$1.99** in 8 years; 10 percent, **$1.95** in 7 years; and 12 percent, **$1.97** in 6 years.

Pretty close, eh?

Problem 6: A Rule of 72 example using real estate

The Rule of 72 is interesting. Let's say your father owns a farm that cost him $200,000 in 1967. He obtains an appraisal in 2007 that indicates the acreage is worth $2 million. Has this been a good investment?

For starters, his investment has doubled 3¼ (3.25) times; once from $200,000 to $400,000; then from $400,000 to $800,000; then from $800,000 to $1,600,000; and then another one-quarter from $1,600,000 to $2,000,000. Now, divide 3.25 into 40, the number of years (2007–1967) he has owned the farm, and you get 13. Finally, divide 72 by 13, which comes to about 5.5 percent. In short, your father's farm has earned the equivalent of 5.5 percent compounded annually since he acquired it. And you figured all that in your head without a calculator or computer.

Problem 7: A Rule of 72 example using stocks

Actually, I used the Rule of 72 recently when helping a financial planner in a lawsuit. One issue had to do with some Berkshire-Hathaway stock that had grown significantly in value over the years (from $2,000 since 1933 to $24 million in 1987). What would be the stock's annual compounded (geometric) rate of return?

Well, over 54 years there had been 13½ (or 13.5) doubles from $2,000 to $24 million. (Go ahead! Count them on your fingers.) Divide 54 years by 13.5. This gives a double every 4 years.

Now for the answer: If a sum doubles every 4 years, it is earning an 18 percent rate of return (72 ÷ 4) compounded annually. That wasn't hard, was it?

Problem 8: The Rule of 72 in retirement income planning

When it comes to a retirement income, use the Rule of 72 this way:

Let's say you are in your mid-30s to mid-40s and plan to retire a millionaire in 20 to 25 years or so, when you are in your 60s. How much must you invest today earning say, 6 percent compounded annually until retirement? To simplify this example, I'll assume you'll reach that milestone in 24 years.

First off, if you refer back to the Rule of 72 list on page 24, you'll see that at 6 percent interest, this money will double twice—every 12 years (72 ÷ 6 equals 12)—over this 24-year period. Now, divide $1 million by two (twice), and you'll get a $250,000 lump sum.

Note: If the rate of return is 9 percent, your money will double three times; once every 8 years. Divide $1 million (by two) three times to reach a $125,000 lump sum. Accordingly, you'll only need a $62,500 lump sum if the rate of return is 12 percent (since this money will double four times—every 6 years).

Goodness! Just find a $62,500, 12 percent investment and you, too, can be a millionaire at age 65. You might even get there with a $125,000, 9 percent investment. (And if you find these investments, let me know where they are!)

Again, all it took to figure this out was some mental arithmetic using the rule of 72. You could do this without a calculator, computer, or even Chart 1.

Note: To quadruple your money, you'll need to double your money twice. For example, a 5 percent earnings rate doubles $100,000 to $200,000 after 14 years; and it will take another 14 years to double again. Your money will triple from $100,000 to $300,000 in about 22 years.

GROWTH ON MONEY SET ASIDE ANNUALLY

We've been studying Chart 1, which shows how a lump sum accumulates given various rates of returns. But retirement income planning frequently involves setting aside smaller yearly amounts, rather than one large lump sum. Take a look at Problems 9 through 11 and note the differences in how money grows through this process.

Problem 9: Saving money systematically and safely at 5 percent

You have about 25 years until retirement and can save $10,000 from an annual bonus each year. How much will there be eventually in the retirement fund? Look at Chart 2 on page 29. One dollar set aside each year, at 5 percent interest, will equal about $50 after 25 years. Similarly, $10,000 invested annually will build to $500,000 ($10,000 × 50).

There's something here that's worth remembering: *If you are about 25 years from retirement and choose a conservative 5 percent accumulation pattern, your input will double over these years.*

So, $10,000 contributed annually for 25 years (a total of $250,000) will grow to $500,000—twice the input. And $20,000 set aside annually (a total of $500,000) will grow to $1 million. (Conversely, to accumulate $500,000 [at 5 percent in annual contributions over 25 years], set aside $250,000 in total or $10,000 each year.)

Note these mathematical relationships. Once more, a series of regular annual contributions invested safely at 5 percent will secure an aggregate double after 25 years.

Problem 10: Saving money systematically and aggressively at 8 percent

Using an "aggressive" 8 percent pattern, how much can you accumulate over 25 years investing, say, $10,000 annually?

Obviously, for a $250,000 assembled input, you will have more than $500,000. How much more? Well, Chart 2 says you'll have $789,540—$10,000 × 78.954 ($800,000 rounded).

What's interesting here is that you'll be earning 3 percent over the 5 percent rate, which is 60 percent more in terms of a percentage increase. Similarly, there will be $800,000 instead of $500,000—also a 60 percent improvement.

Get it? Instead of $500,000 (earning 5 percent), there is $800,000 (earning 8 percent).

The numbers relate perfectly. Five percent is to 8 percent as $500,000 is to $800,000! That is, over a 25-year period.

Amazingly simple! Isn't it?

Problem 11: Saving money systematically and "super aggressively" at 9 percent and 10 percent

Now we know a $10,000 annual investment over 25 years will grow to $500,000 (at 5 percent) and $800,000 (at 8 percent). What will happen to this savings pattern if the earnings rate is 9 percent? Or 10 percent?

Seemingly, there will be about $900,000. Or $1 million. Actually, the numbers from Chart 2 are $923,240 and $1,081,820—a little more than $900,000 and $1 million, but close enough.

hart 2

he Results of Various Rates of Return on One Dollar per Annum,
aved at the Beginning of *Each* Year (BOY)

					Rate				
ar	3%	4%	5%	6%	7%	8%	9%	10%	12%
1	$1.030	$1.040	$1.050	$1.060	$1.070	$1.080	$1.090	$1.100	$1.120
2	2.091	2.122	2.152	2.184	2.215	2.246	2.278	2.310	2.374
3	3.183	3.246	3.310	3.375	3.440	3.506	3.573	3.641	3.779
4	4.309	4.416	4.526	4.637	4.751	4.867	4.985	5.105	5.353
5	5.468	5.633	5.802	5.975	6.153	6.336	5.052	6.716	7.115
6	6.662	6.898	7.142	7.394	7.654	7.923	8.200	8.487	9.089
7	7.892	8.214	8.549	8.897	9.260	9.637	10.028	10.436	11.300
8	9.159	9.583	10.027	10.491	10.978	11.488	12.021	12.579	13.776
9	10.463	11.006	11.578	12.181	12.816	13.487	14.193	14.937	16.549
0	11.807	12.486	13.207	13.972	14.784	15.645	16.560	17.531	19.655
1	13.192	14.026	14.917	15.870	16.888	17.977	19.141	20.384	23.133
2	14.618	15.627	16.713	17.882	19.141	20.495	21.953	23.523	27.029
3	16.086	17.292	18.599	20.015	22.550	23.215	25.019	26.975	31.393
4	17.599	19.024	20.579	22.276	24.129	26.152	28.361	30.772	36.280
5	19.157	20.825	22.657	24.673	26.888	29.324	32.003	34.950	41.753
6	20.762	22.698	24.840	27.213	29.840	32.750	35.974	39.545	47.884
7	22.414	26.671	27.132	29.906	32.999	36.450	40.301	44.599	54.750
8	24.117	28.778	29.539	32.760	36.379	40.446	45.018	50.159	62.440
9	25.870	30.969	32.066	35.786	39.995	44.762	50.160	56.275	71.052
0	27.676	30.969	34.719	38.993	43.865	49.423	55.765	63.002	80.699
1	29.537	33.248	37.505	42.392	48.006	54.457	61.875	70.403	91.503
2	31.453	35.618	40.430	45.996	52.436	59.893	68.532	78.543	103.603
3	33.426	38.083	43.502	49.816	57.177	65.765	75.790	87.497	117.155
4	35.459	40.646	46.727	53.865	62.249	72.106	83.701	97.347	132.334
5	37.553	43.312	50.113	58.156	67.676	78.954	92.324	108.182	149.334
6	39.710	46.084	53.669	62.706	73.484	86.351	101.723	120.100	168.374
7	41.931	48.968	57.403	67.528	79.698	94.339	111.968	133.210	189.699
8	44.219	51.966	61.323	72.640	86.347	102.966	123.135	147.631	213.583
9	46.575	55.085	65.439	78.058	93.461	112.283	135.308	163.494	240.333
0	49.003	58.328	69.761	83.802	101.073	122.346	148.575	180.943	270.293
1	51.502	61.701	74.299	89.890	109.218	133.214	163.037	200.138	303.848
2	54.078	65.210	79.064	96.343	117.933	144.951	178.800	221.252	341.429
3	56.730	68.858	84.067	103.184	127.259	157.627	195.982	244.477	383.521
4	59.462	72.652	89.320	110.435	137.237	171.317	214.711	270.024	430.663
5	62.276	76.598	94.836	118.121	147.913	186.102	235.125	298.127	483.463

A review: Let's say we have a saver in his late 30s or early 40s who can earn 5 percent (safe) and 8 percent (aggressive) invested returns. This man will retire in 25 years or so in his mid-60s. (Or, he could be in his late 40s or early 50s and seeking to retire in his mid-70s.) Know that a $10,000 annual, systematic savings pattern over this period will double one's aggregate input to $500,000 at 5 percent. In proportion to an 8 percent rate, it will increase the total to $800,000. At 9 percent and 10 percent, it will assemble something more than $900,000 and $1,000,000.

This is meaningful numbers trivia. It gives a pretty good idea of what lies ahead in a creative retirement income plan. See? You don't need a calculator or computer to come close to the actual figures—only Charts 1 and 2 and a little practice. And if the numbers seem high, they probably aren't. With prospects of inflation, you really could need a bushel of money someday.

Let's start now on the series of exercises that will help you determine how much annual income you will need in retirement and how much retirement income capital is required to get you there.

Problem 12: Saving to maintain your standard of living

Now, some tough questions and a little more math as well. Let's say your salary is $50,000 annually. You set aside $10,000 annually at 5 percent on the way to a comfy $500,000 retirement kitty in 25 years. Will it really be enough? Or possibly too much?

Maybe yes, maybe no. In truth, there are many perspectives on this and just as many ways to calculate a nest egg to pay a retirement income.

One approach uses the simple idea of replacement costs. In the *Complete Retirement Guidebook*, authors Glenn Ruffenach and Kelly Greene give credit to Charles Farrell for his "one-minute drill." He suggests the following: First, multiply your current income (income just before retirement) by .80 (80 percent) to assemble the income needed. Then multiply your current income by 12 to reach your savings needed for retirement.

Example: You are age 65—just 1 year away from that first income check, with a salary of $80,000. Then, (a) 80 percent × $80,000 is $64,000, and (b) 12 × $80,000 is $960,000 (which is what Mr. Farrell says will cover that $64,000 income check).

Obviously, Mr. Farrell thinks that 80 percent of "final salary" is reasonable in retirement. (I tend to agree, but if there is debt and aggressive spending ahead, it's possible that 100 percent or more of final salary is better.) From what I have read, he seems to presume that (a) you can earn 6 to 7 percent on your kitty, (b) you want to pass what's left to heirs, and (c) inflation isn't an important factor. It's possible to adjust for any of these assumptions. Shortly, we'll do just that.

Give credit to Mr. Farrell. But your personal circumstances will normally lead to far different numbers than he suggests.

First off, you will surely have lower expenses in retirement (mortgage paid off, college funded, etc.). That's why experts say it is reasonable to have merely 80 percent of final salary as an income goal. At least the target for an 80 percent income is less than for a 100 percent income. So let's go with this; it can be changed later if more is affordable. Everything is adjusted for inflation, of course. If so, how much capital will you need to do the job?

Don't worry about answering this. Remember the challenge I set for you at the beginning of this chapter? We are about to explore—in detail—the process that will give you your annual income and retirement capital goals. Here goes!

We start with a $50,000 salary (and the 80 percent test); 80 percent of $50,000 is a $40,000 income in retirement. But we have been setting aside $10,000 a year for retirement—at age 65, we'll no longer need to do that. So let's subtract this $10,000 in savings to get a current spendable income of $40,000. Then, multiply 80 percent × $40,000 and obtain $32,000 annually as the retirement income goal at age 65.

This plan gives credit for what you save, and it makes sense. It is a little difficult to calculate quickly. (On the one hand, settle in on a savings figure [$10,000 here]; on the other, you must glean 80 percent of spendable income [$32,000 here].) And the kitty at retirement might not be right on target to pay $32,000. These are interdependent factors, and some judgment and trial and error is necessary.

Let's test whether $10,000 at 5 percent annually will grow sufficiently to give a $32,000 income in retirement.

For openers, seemingly a kitty of $640,000 is necessary ($640,000 × .05 equals $32,000)! Viewed another way, $32,000 × 20 (100 ÷ 5) also equals $640,000.

Adjust for inflation, of course.

Problem 13: Saving toward an 80 percent income goal adjusted for inflation

Use Chart 1. With inflation at 3½ percent, a current $40,000 income will just about double to $80,000 in 20 to 25 years (20 years × a 3½ percent inflation rate equals 70). In other words, to keep pace with inflation, that first income check at, say, age 66 must be $64,000 ($80,000 × 80 percent) and not $32,000. You also need to increase your retirement income capital from $640,000 to about $1,280,000.

Is that even enough for over 20 to 25 years in retirement? Not quite! Since you can expect inflation during all of your retirement years, an income needs to keep pace and grow gradually from $64,000 to about $122,000 (20 × 3½ equals 70), which is actually a median income of nearly $89,000 annually in retirement. (See Illustration 1.)

Illustration 1
An Annual Income of $64,000 EOY Increasing at 3½ Percent Annually

Year	EOY Income
1	$64,000
2	66,000
3	68,000
4	71,000
5	73,000
6	76,000
7	78,000
8	81,000
9	84,000
10	87,000
	($88,500–$89,000 rounded)
11	90,000
12	93,000
13	96,000
14	100,000
15	103,000
16	107,000
17	110,000
18	114,000
19	118,000
20	122,000

The bottom line: Conceivably, you could need to increase your retirement income capital again from $1,280,000 to about $1,800,000 ($89,000 × 20). If you amass that amount—$1,800,000—and you put it into a savings vehicle that pays 5 percent interest consistently, it will pay you $64,000 the first year (when you are age 65), increasing to $122,000 in the 20th year (when you are age 85). This would give you an $89,000 median annual income. (And $89,000 is right at 5 percent of $1,800,000.) What is left when you die will presumably pass to children and grandchildren as an inheritance.

The questions and answers get tougher. Do your heirs really need that kind of money? With steady jobs and good educations, could they fend for themselves without this inheritance? Could you leave them other assets, perhaps life insurance? Can you actually look at this retirement fund as yours and yours alone to spend? After all, this might be better than going broke and moving in with the kids someday. Look at it from their perspectives.

Think seriously about income planning. Ask "Who makes those rules that guarantee the kids a nifty stipend?" The answers may lead you to say truly, "I'm spending my children's inheritance!" If so, don't feel alone; you and a great many others may need to do that to survive.

"SPENDING DOWN": AMORTIZATION OVER TIME

Problem 14: Saving toward an 80 percent of spendable income, inflation-adjusted retirement kitty on an amortized basis

As I mentioned earlier, the process of "spending down" a kitty in retirement is called amortizing, where your remaining principal continues to earn interest.

Chart 3 on page 35 is an amortization chart that "liquidates" capital over a number of years. It shows that for every $1,000 paid annually in retirement, a specific amount on hand at the beginning of the spend-down period is necessary. Each level payment is a mixture of principal and interest—something similar to a level-payment home mortgage, where someone is paid for use of his money. At the end of the payout period, an initial lump sum will be gone. (If the prospect of "going broke" someday seems frightening, read about payout annuities beginning on page 133. I'll give some solutions there that will soothe your fears.)

Example: In Chart 3, go to the 5% column and scroll down to the 20th year to see $12,462. If $12,462 amortized will pay $1,000 annually over 20 years, then roughly $1,100,000 (see Illustration 2) can pay out an $89,000 median income (12.462 × $89,000). Not $1,800,000 in capital—just $1,100,000! And, I emphasize, *just* $1,100,000. The money will run out in two decades, but you'll lower

Chart 3

Lump Sums that Amortize $1,000 Paid at the End of Each Year (EOY)
at Various Rates of Return

Rate

Year	5%	6%	7%	8%	9%	10%
1	$ 952	$ 943	$ 935	$ 926	$ 917	$ 909
2	1,859	1,833	1,808	1,783	1,759	1,736
3	2,723	2,673	2,624	2,577	2,531	2,487
4	3,546	3,465	3,387	3,312	3,240	3,170
5	4,329	4,212	4,100	3,993	3,890	3,791
6	5,076	4,917	4,767	4,623	4,486	4,355
7	5,786	5,582	5,389	5,206	5,033	4,868
8	6,463	6,210	5,971	5,747	5,535	5,335
9	7,108	6,802	6,515	6,247	5,995	5,759
10	7,722	7,360	7,024	6,710	6,418	6,145
11	8,306	7,887	7,499	7,139	6,805	6,495
12	8,863	8,384	7,943	7,536	7,161	6,814
13	9,394	8,853	8,358	7,904	7,487	7,103
14	9,899	9,295	8,745	8,244	7,786	7,367
15	10,380	9,712	9,108	8,559	8,061	7,606
16	10,838	10,106	9,447	8,851	8,313	7,824
17	11,274	10,477	9,763	9,122	8,544	8,022
18	11,690	10,828	10,059	9,372	8,756	8,201
19	12,085	11,158	10,336	9,604	8,950	8,365
20	12,462	11,470	10,594	9,818	9,129	8,514
21	12,821	11,764	10,836	10,017	9,292	8,649
22	13,163	12,042	11,061	10,201	9,442	8,772
23	13,489	12,303	11,272	10,371	8,580	8,883
24	13,799	12,550	11,469	10,529	9,707	8,985
25	14,094	12,783	11,654	10,675	9,823	9,077
26	14,375	13,003	11,826	10,810	9,929	9,161
27	14,643	13,211	11,987	10,935	10,027	9,237
28	14,898	13,406	12,137	11,051	10,116	9,307
29	15,141	13,590	12,278	11,158	10,198	9,370
30	15,372	13,765	12,409	11,258	10,274	9,427

Illustration 2

$1,100,000 Spent Down over 20 Years, Assuming a 3½% Inflation Rate

Year	Sum at EOY at 5% Interest	Annual Income EOY Increasing at 3½%	Sum on Hand BOY Next Year After Annual Income Is Withdrawn
1	$1,155,000	$64,000	$1,090,000
2	1,145,000	66,000	1,080,000
3	1,135,000	68,000	1,070,000
4	1,120,000	71,000	1,050,000
5	1,100,000	73,000	1,030,000
6	1,080,000	76,000	1,000,000
7	1,055,000	78,000	980,000
8	1,025,000	81,000	940,000
9	990,000	84,000	910,000
10	950,000	87,000	870,000
		($88,500*–$89,000 rounded)	
11	910,000	90,000	820,000
12	860,000	93,000	770,000
13	800,000	96,000	710,000
14	750,000	100,000	650,000
15	680,000	103,000	580,000
16	610,000	107,000	500,000
17	530,000	110,000	420,000
18	440,000	114,000	320,000
19	340,000	118,000	220,000
20	230,000	122,000	110,000

* A median income of $88,500 ($87,000 + 90,000 ÷ 2) over a 20-year period.

your retirement income capital goal all the way to $1,100,000—a reduction of nearly 40 percent ($700,000).

Problem 15: Building in a Social Security factor

Reflect. We began an income discussion on the basis of a $50,000 salary and 80 percent of $40,000 in net spendable income as a goal roughly after 25 years. Adjusted for inflation, we reached $89,000 as a median income in retirement from a $1,800,000 income kitty.

Finally, we reduced that capital to $1,100,000 and amortized it between ages 66 and 85. (Again, see Illustration 2.)

We can do better by assuming that Social Security will be there in retirement. That may be a lot to ask, but somehow I feel the system will preserve this income—or at least some of it.

If your final gross annual earnings at age 65 are $100,000 (which is $50,000 adjusted for 3½ percent inflation in 20 to 25 years) let's use something like $22,000 (which comes out to nearly 25 percent of $89,000) as a Social Security stipend. Under present Social Security rules, this too will be adjusted for inflation over the years. Accordingly, that would bring a $1,100,000 retirement kitty down by 25 percent to about $800,000.

Now, $500,000 of retirement capital seems more practical and attainable. Here's why: You'll fill in the $300,000 gap ($800,000 less $500,000) with the concepts I'll outline in Problem 16.

Problem 16: Filling in a retirement income gap

Obviously, $500,000 is less than $800,000—so we have a $300,000 shortfall. At least we know what we are up against. Fortunately, there are some options. Try the following ideas to bring these numbers closer together:

1. **Save more now.** Set aside more money toward a lump sum at retirement age. We began our discussion by assuming a $10,000 contribution at 5 percent toward a $500,000 retirement kitty after about 24 to 25 years. By adding, say, $2,000 (20 percent more) annually toward this goal, the lump sum will grow by 20 percent to $600,000. This alone will reduce the $300,000 shortfall to $200,000 ($800,000 less $600,000).

2. **Plan to spend less in retirement.** Reduce an income goal from 80 percent to 60 percent or even 50 percent of final net

income. Earlier, I introduced the 80 percent of net income test, instead of 100 percent of net income. I reasoned that your income needs in retirement might be less (mortgage paid off, education funded, etc.). To fill in an income gap, consider a lesser percentage—60 percent or so. Personally, I don't like this idea all that much. But something is certainly better than nothing. And a capital requirement will be lowered proportionately. (For instance, if 80 percent of net income at 5 percent interest requires an $800,000, 20-year income kitty, 60 percent of net income at 5 percent will lower the goal to $600,000 [60/80 × $800,000].)

3. **Choose investments with more market risk before retirement.** Change the assumed accumulation interest rate pre-retirement from 5 percent to a higher return. Here is an example. In Problem 10, I referred to Chart 2 and explained that $10,000 at 8 percent annually gives $800,000 (actually $789,540) after 25 years. (It also grows to about $500,000 after merely 20 years, since $10,000 × 49.423 equals $494,230.) And then, there will be a gain of about $100,000 for each extra percentage point. Here are figures from Chart 2:

After 25 Years	Multiplying Factor	Accumulation (Rounded)
$10,000 annually at 5%	50.113	$ 500,000
$10,000 annually at 6%	58.156	$ 580,000 (600,000)
$10,000 annually at 7%	67.676	$ 680,000 (700,000)
$10,000 annually at 8%	78.954	$ 790,000 (800,000)
$10,000 annually at 9%	92.324	$ 920,000 (900,000)
$10,000 annually at 10%	108.182	$1,080,000 (1,100,000)

In other words, if you can earn 8 percent over a 25-year period, you'll have $800,000. And there won't be a gap anymore.

A word of caution: Nowadays, it seems that you take on market risk by seeking more than a 4 or 5 percent annual return offered in U.S. Treasuries. There's probably not much at 6 percent or 7 percent, but there is some. Always discuss risk assumptions with a financial advisor.

4. **Select investments with more market risk after retirement.** Choose a more aggressive amortization interest rate in the retirement payout phase. In Problem 14, I introduced Chart 3, which gives lump sums necessary to pay out $1,000 annually over a number of years. For instance, Chart 3 shows about $1,100,000 is enough at 5 percent to pay out (amortize) $89,000 during 20 more years, in retirement. Recall also that $800,000 is our retirement kitty, once we assume a yearly Social Security income of $22,000 and reduce $89,000 to $67,000. Use Chart 3 to consider the possibilities.

Actual Capital Needed to "Amortize Out" a $67,000 Level Annual Income over 20- and 25-Year Periods

Lump Sums (Rounded)	Annual Income
$840,000 at 5% – 20 years (12,462 × $67)	$67,000
$770,000 at 6% – 20 years	$67,000
$710,000 at 7% – 20 years	$67,000
$660,000 at 8% – 20 years	$67,000
$610,000 at 9% – 20 years	$67,000
$570,000 at 10% – 20 years	$67,000
$910,000 at 5% – 25 years (14,094 × $67)	$67,000
$850,000 at 6% – 25 years	$67,000
$780,000 at 7% – 25 years	$67,000
$720,000 at 8% – 25 years	$67,000
$660,000 at 9% – 25 years	$67,000
$610,000 at 10% – 25 years	$67,000

For example, if you accumulate only $500,000 pre-retirement (and can earn 8 percent over 20 years in retirement), you'll only have a $160,000 shortfall ($660,000 less

$500,000). Isn't it interesting how relatively small increases in interest rates can significantly decrease what's necessary to amortize a given income in retirement? This is the power of money compounding over the years (as you liquidate capital and earn interest on what remains of that capital).

5. **Plan to retire later.** Push the income date to age 68, age 70, or even later. We usually think in terms of retiring in our mid-60s. This idea probably originated in the 1930s when Social Security began. However, life expectancies are increasing and in 20 to 25 years, someone age 70 should comfortably have a 50-50 chance of living 20 more years, until age 90 or so. For planning purposes, another 5 years of accumulation can do wonders. For example: At age 40, you begin setting aside $10,000 annually at 5 percent toward a $500,000 lump sum at age 65. Give 5 extra years of accumulation until age 70, and you'll have nearly $700,000. In other words, $10,000 × $69,676; please see Chart 2. If the lump sum goal is $800,000 (see Problem 15), a $100,000 shortfall—$800,000 minus $700,000—is much better than $800,000 less $500,000.

My recommendation: Anytime there is an income shortfall in planning, build in a later retirement age. Coupled with other fill-in-the-gap ideas, this will go a long way in establishing a realistic retirement income program.

The important thing is to get grounded about planning for retirement. The methods in this chapter will get you within range of where you want to go. Then fine-tune the details with your financial planner.

Let's return again to the exercise I gave you at the beginning of this chapter and Problems 12 through16. In summary, you first calculate an annual contribution toward a retirement income kitty, say $10,000. As I described earlier in Problem 9, a $10,000 annual contribution set aside at 5 percent interest will grow to $500,000 in 25 years. We could assume that $500,000 is also your preliminary retirement income capital goal. But this is my number. Now it's time to use your figures. Here are the six steps:

1. Determine how much you can set aside to accumulate at 5 percent interest toward your retirement income capital goal.

2. Calculate 80 percent of your net income goal. (Or determine an income goal that will maintain your current standard of living—for starters, 80 percent of current income minus income used for retirement savings.)

3. Adjust that income by a 3½ percent inflation factor on the way to retirement. Increase your retirement income capital (your kitty) accordingly.

4. Increase that income gradually to plan for inflation in retirement. Increase your retirement income capital once more.

5. Reduce the final lump sum kitty (about 35 to 40 percent) over 20 years in retirement by amortizing or spending down your retirement income capital.

6. Give yourself a portion of final income from Social Security. But be reasonable: Social Security probably won't pay much more than $30,000 or so in annual income. Reduce the lump sum you determined in Step 5 accordingly.

Compare the sum you will actually need for retirement income (Step 6) with your original retirement capital target (Step 1). Then, for planning purposes, make adjustments to fill in the gaps between these amounts.

Congratulations—you've done it! Good planning.

Now that you know how much capital you'll need for 20 or 25 years in retirement, let's look next at creative strategies that will keep taxes to an absolute minimum so your savings can build more quickly toward your retirement goal.

SIX STEPS TO GET YOUR RETIREMENT INCOME PLANNING OFF TO A GOOD START

---

1. Stay positive. Don't get sucked into all the negative news about Social Security, the economy, and so on. Instead, shut the door, turn off the TV, and sit down with a financial planner who understands present and future values and the planning ideas in this book.

2. Build top lines of credit. Look at good credit as an asset. It will allow you to borrow enough to tide yourself over in an emergency.

3. Get comfortable with the Internet and e-mail. Share your ideas with a cyberspace financial support group for people looking to build a quality income in retirement. If you are unfamiliar with the computer, take a class and get started. Push yourself just a bit here; you'll eventually have fun with this.

4. Keep a "NOTES" file where you can assemble questions to share with your financial planning team.

5. Go to seminars, workshops, and courses on retirement income planning. Learn to be discerning in a rapidly changing financial world.

6. Don't be afraid to share ideas about money with friends. I've found that they share your interests, and want to discuss their views with you.

FROM TAXABLE INTO TAX FREE

A fine is a tax for doing wrong,
A tax is a fine for doing well.
—*Anonymous*

It's one thing to save for retirement; it's another to do it *effectively*. To me, that means putting your serious retirement money in IRAs, qualified plans, annuities, cash value life insurance polices—even your home. These are the savings vehicles that can offer both protection from claimants and tax advantages to build on.

In this chapter, we'll look at strategies that can keep your retirement savings sheltered from income taxes to the *full* extent allowed by law. (In the next chapter, we'll cover asset protection.) Understanding the tax implications of any savings strategy is important because tax savings can add up to big gains over time.

This chapter is also somewhat math intensive. If you prefer, just skim it for now, or skip it entirely. But do come back to it later. You'll definitely want to learn how to save on taxes by putting your savings in instruments that allow tax deductions on contributions, or tax-deferral on contributions and earnings, or even tax-free growth and distributions.

Think of it this way: the less you pay in taxes, the higher your *actual* rate of return. Strategies that save taxes could make a 5 percent rate of return seem higher than 7 or 8 percent from a riskier investment that has no tax savings. In savings instruments where money can grow tax-free, interest builds even more quickly on principal that otherwise might have been lost to taxes.

You always want to consider the tax features when you are looking at a savings vehicle, or comparing one to another. Ask: Can it give a tax deduction on earnings you contribute? Does it offer tax deferral? Tax free growth? What will the tax bite be when you withdraw the money?

Train yourself to consider this each time you explore savings or investment possibilities. Aim to get as close as you can to the Holy Grail of retirement income planning: a fully tax-sheltered program. In other words, in the *ideal* situation, you'd claim a tax deduction on money you put into the savings vehicle, have the money grow tax free, and withdraw it tax free. You wouldn't pay *any* taxes ever on interest or principal.

That said, let me be honest. Under current tax law, this Holy Grail *isn't* possible—although I think Congress should consider laws that make it so. You can get awfully close; I will show you how later in this chapter.

Still, it is useful to imagine the ideal—if only to compare available strategies against it and see which get closest. Let's simplify things by using a common set of facts in all of the examples that follow. Let's say you are age 45 and pay a 30 percent tax rate when you combine federal and state taxes. You have $5,000 to save annually at the beginning of the year in a 20-year savings program that earns 5 percent interest compounded annually. At the end of the 20th year, you'd have roughly $174,000.

If you could achieve the Holy Grail, you would claim a full $5,000 tax deduction on each $5,000 annual contribution, making your net output only $3,500. (That's because you'd save $1,500 on taxes on some other income.) And—in 20 years—you would also be able to withdraw your money without ever having to pay taxes on any of it. That means that 20 years out, you'd have $174,000 tax free. Not bad for an annual contribution of $3,500. In fact, if you were to divide the sum available after 20 years—$174,000—by the net annual input—$3,500—you'd arrive at a quotient of 49.7. (A quotient is the number of times one number is contained in another. For our purposes here, the higher the quotient, the better.) In this case, a 49.7 percent quotient is incredible! It effectively raises a compounded rate of return from 5 percent to 8 percent. (See Chart 2 in chapter 1, where $1 saved each year for 20 years builds to $49.42 if it constantly earns an 8 percent return.)

Keep this 49.7 quotient in mind because we will use it as a point of comparison for strategies that *are* possible under current tax law.

SECTION I: THE ABCs OF TAX-ADVANTAGED SAVINGS PROGRAMS

In this section, I will walk you through four possibilities (A through D). You will see how the differences affect the net yield on a savings program that uses my same common set of facts: a $5,000 annual contribution for 20 years into a savings vehicle that provides a steady 5 percent return compounded annually, building to $174,000. The combined state/federal tax bracket is 30 percent.

To keep things simple, I will cover just the tax features first. In the next section, I'll identify nine specific savings vehicles that can give you one—or some combination—of these tax features. I will also rate each on a scale of 1 to 10, with 10 being the most favorable result.

Let's keep our terminology straight as well. I'm referring to 5 percent over 20 years as a "geometric mean" rate of return compounded annually—rather than an arithmetic rate of return. (See "The Difference Between an Arithmetic and Geometric Rate of Return," next.)

THE DIFFERENCE BETWEEN AN ARITHMETIC AND GEOMETRIC RATE OF RETURN

In finance, a rate of return can be expressed in different ways, such as an *arithmetic rate of return* or a *geometric rate of return.*

Here's an example of the latter: $100,000 that reaches $265,300 steadily over 20 years earns a 5 percent *geometric* rate of return. That's $100,000 compounding at 5 percent consistently over the 20-year period.

An *arithmetic* rate of return is different. To illustrate this, let's say you had a painting valued at $100,000 hanging on a wall in your house for 19 years. Until you sell it, it arguably is still worth $100,000 at the 19th year. At the end of the 20th year, you sell it for, say, $265,300 (an increase of 165 percent from $100,000 to $265,300 during that year).

What is the painting's arithmetic rate of return? It is 19 years at zero percent and 1 year at 165 percent, for an average of 8.25 percent (165 ÷ 20). Therefore, its arithmetic rate of return is 8.25 percent. Its geometric rate of return is still 5 percent, however.

Here's another example: Over a 9-year period, you double $1,000 to $2,000, earning +50 percent, −10 percent, +20 percent, +3 percent, +6 percent, +4 percent, +4 percent, +4 percent, and zero rates of return. Your arithmetic (average) rate of return is 9 percent (81 ÷ 9). Your geometric (steady) rate of return is 8 percent; that's because money doubles under the Rule of 72 in 9 years at a steady 8 percent. Fun, isn't it?

So, when someone says to you, "That investment earned 5 percent over 20 years," you should ask, whether they mean arithmetically—where you take an average of all percentage returns—or geometrically, which is the internal compounding rate that I use in this chapter.

Scenario A: Taxable Conventional Savings

Let's say you have the same $5,000 to save annually—for the next 20 years—but you *don't* consider the tax implications. Instead, you put the money into a conventional savings instrument (like a treasury or certificate of deposit) that pays 5 percent compounded annually. The government won't give you a tax deduction on money you put into a personal conventional savings vehicle *and* you'll have to pay income taxes on the 5 percent in earnings.

This changes things quite a bit. Since you have to pay income taxes of 30 percent on annual earnings, your net earnings rate drops from 5 percent to 3.5 percent (which is 5 percent reduced by 30 percent). After 20 years, you'll only have $146,000 after taxes—a far cry from $174,000. If you divide the sum available—$146,000—by the net annual input of $5,000, you get a quotient of only 29.2. Frankly, that's terrible. It is *not* a good way to efficiently accumulate retirement income capital.

You can do just a little better if you use $5,000 annually to buy, say, a capital appreciation mutual fund where your 5 percent return is taxed fully at a 15 percent capital gains rate each year. The government won't give you a tax deduction either, but at least the annual income tax on earnings will be less, which makes the actual return closer to 4.25 percent after taxes are deducted.

This savings program would give you $160,000 in 20 years (for a quotient of 32). That's a little better than the 29.2 quotient for conventional savings vehicles, but not enough in my book.

Scenario B: No Tax Deduction with Tax Deferral on Earnings

Let's say you opt for a savings vehicle that features tax deferral. Over 20 years, the same $5,000 in annual contributions would build a profit of $74,000 and accumulate to $174,000 pre-tax. You would net $152,000—a quotient of 30.4 ($152,000÷$5,000)—after paying $22,000 in ordinary income taxes in your 30 percent bracket. Here, too, you could invest in capital assets and pay only 15 percent in capital gains taxes on $74,000. That would cut your tax obligation to $11,000 and increase your net to $163,000—a quotient of 32.6. As you can see, the net results for this tax-deferred savings program—$152,000 or $163,000 for a capital asset—are better than the $146,000 and $160,000 you'd net using conventional savings vehicles (because you earn interest on tax dollars that you *didn't* pay over the years).

This shows you what happens when you gain use of tax money you don't pay the IRS. And we're just getting started.

Scenario C: Tax Deduction with Tax Deferral on Earnings

What if you were to put that $5,000 into a savings vehicle instead that allows you to get a tax deduction on contributions—and tax-deferred growth? Because you get a 30 percent tax deduction on your contribution, your annual net input is only $3,500 (after $1,500 in tax savings). After 20 years, the fund will build to $174,000. Once you cash out, you'll pay $52,000 in taxes (30 percent of $174,000) and net $122,000. A $3,500 net annual input that grows to $122,000 is certainly better than $5,000 that becomes $152,000 or $163,000. Prove it by dividing $122,000 by $3,500, which gives you a quotient of about 34.8—which is even better than the 32.6 quotient in scenario B. (Again, the higher the quotient, the better the result.)

Now you are getting somewhere. Can you do better? Maybe!

Scenario D: No Tax Deduction with Tax Free Earnings

How do savings vehicles that offer tax-deductible contributions with tax deferral on earnings compare with those that don't give a tax deduction but do feature tax free earnings? It might surprise you that the quotient is the same.

In a tax free savings program, you'd gross $174,000 after 20 years and get a quotient of 34.8 ($174,000 ÷ 5,000), the same as scenario C. So, with all other things being equal, a "no tax deduction with tax free earnings" program is identical to a "tax deduction with tax-deferred earnings" program.

What does all this mean? First, know that the Holy Grail of retirement income planning is to get as close as possible to "tax deductible with tax free earnings." But most anything—except a taxable conventional savings plan—is acceptable. Even that could work if you simply need a liquid emergency fund; at least it's better than nothing. To get optimal results, you must select the right structure. In the next section, I'll discuss what's available and how to make a selection.

SECTION II: PRACTICAL APPLICATIONS: NINE SAVINGS VEHICLES THAT OFFER TAX ADVANTAGES

We've been looking at how differences in tax features affect net yields. Next, I will match one or more savings vehicles to each category, and rate each one on a scale of 1 to 10. Let's see how close they come to the Holy Grail of financial planning, which again, is associated with a quotient of 49.7.

Scenario A: Taxable Conventional Savings (Using CDs, Treasury Bonds or Notes, etc.)

It's easy to find savings programs that don't have tax advantages. All you have to do is acquire a debt obligation (treasury bond or note, certificate of deposit [CD], money market instrument, corporate bond, or even a bond mutual fund). Most earnings on each of these are taxable as ordinary income.

As I showed you in scenario A of Section I "The ABCs of Tax-Advantaged Savings Programs," you'd net $146,000 if you put $5,000 each year in any of these. Your quotient would be a mere 29.2.

If you have your money in this conventional savings plan now, here's how you might improve things—and get yourself a guaranteed lifelong income in retirement. Consider cashing in the $146,000 and acquiring a *single premium immediate annuity* (SPIA), which can assure a lifelong income. (See chapter 7 for more on SPIAs.) The sooner, the better. All policies have guaranteed annuity purchase rates (amounts of income monthly per $1,000 of cash value). Since the average lifespan is getting longer, there's a good chance that a policy purchased today—to provide income later—will have a better annuity purchase rate than a contract acquired, say, 20 years from now.

Of course, you could liquidate your savings kitty yourself, but I don't recommend this. Let me show you why: Let's assume you arrange to have the $146,000 paid out evenly over 20 years—in installments of about $11,500 at the end of each year—while the remaining principal continues to earn 5 percent interest. (I'll call this liquidation process "self-amortization.") That will give you a total payout of $230,000. In the first year, your taxable income will be $7,300 (5 percent × $146,000). The $4,200 remainder of the payout will be a tax free return of principal. Over time, the taxable portion of each $11,500 payment will decrease gradually until the 20th year, when a final distribution is mostly principal and tax free. This is inefficient tax-wise when you compare the results to a SPIA, which offers level taxation. (I will demonstrate this next.)

Here are the other disadvantages: CDs have surrender charges, a treasury has market value adjustments, and both have limited liquidity. So when you consider these drawbacks along with the fact that conventional savings instruments can't give you a lifetime income or creditor protection, or assistance in managing a daunting self-amortization program, it becomes apparent that these aren't savings vehicles of choice in a core retirement income program. Know that they might not lock in a competitive interest rate either.

Since these are better than nothing, I'd rate them a 2 or 3 on a scale of 1 to 10.

Scenario B-1: No Tax Deduction with Tax Deferral on Earnings (a Cash Value Life Insurance Policy)

There are a few savings vehicles that offer tax deferral. One is a cash value life insurance policy that will be surrendered—or cashed in. (For the purposes of this comparison, let's assume it will be cashed in after 20 years.) This is *not* a great strategy. Let me show you why.

First, you would get a lesser return than 5 percent after paying mortality costs and expenses. It is reasonable to assume, for example, that when these costs are subtracted, a 5 percent return might be reduced to about 4 percent, on average. Second, you'll pay 30 percent taxes at once on the accumulated profit. Third, you'll have to liquidate what's left in retirement. Fourth, to obtain full control over the cash values, you will have to cash out—and that removes the money from any creditor and tax-protected environments. The policy's guaranteed annuity income purchase rates are foregone as well. Simply put, in the 20th year, you will be trading these advantages for a new program that may be inferior to your old policy.

Because of all of this, I'd rate this strategy only a 3 or 4 on a scale of 1 to 10.

Scenario B-2: No Tax Deduction with Tax Deferral on Earnings (an Annual Premium Commercial Annuity Policy)

A commercial accumulation—or deferred—annuity policy (see chapter 6 for more on these) is the better way to go, if you want a savings vehicle that offers tax-deferred growth on tax-paid earnings.

To keep everything consistent with our common set of facts, let's imagine you use the annual $5,000 set-asides to pay a portion each year of a $100,000 premium for an annual premium accumulation annuity policy, rather than pay $100,000 all at once for a *single* premium accumulation annuity earning 5 percent interest. Over the 20 years, this annuity policy will accumulate cash values of $174,000—and then pay out income in retirement. (If you structure it properly, it can also make payments to your heirs, after you die.)

Observations:

- What will you have if income payments from your annuity begin at the end of the 21st year, when you are age 66? At 5 percent interest on the unpaid balance, the annual level annuity payment from $174,000 over a 20-year period will be about $8 per thousand or $14,000 level each year (8 × 174). (Alternately, a monthly payment of $1,150 would be possible.) If interest rates at payout are less—perhaps 4 percent— you'll still receive $12,700 annually or $1,040 monthly.

- How is each annual payment (at 5 percent interest) taxed? Since you've paid-in $100,000 and expect to receive $280,000 ($14,000 × 20 payments), a fraction (exclusion ratio) is formed—$100,000 ÷ $280,000 = 0.36. Therefore, roughly 36 percent of each payment is tax free and 64 percent is taxable. Accordingly, as a $14,000 check is deposited to your bank account, the carrier sends a Form 1099R indicating that for *each* of 20 years about $5,000 (36 percent × $14,000) is tax free and $9,000 is taxable. After about 20 years, your $100,000 contribution is used up and payments to you cease.

- Self-amortization, which I explained in scenario A, taxes distributions LIFO (last in taxable earnings, first out). Compare that with SPIAs, which are taxed based on a *level* percentage. This leveling is advantageous. It effectively raises an interest rate factor over 20 years by about 10 percent—say 5.0 to 5.5 percent. The reason is that compared with LIFO taxation, a level exclusion ratio gives some "use" of tax money during the early years.

- Will the payout be adjusted if you want a *lifetime* income? Yes! To assure that lifelong payments will continue past the 20th year (when you turn 85), the annual payment throughout will be less—say about $12,100 instead of $14,000. (The income decreases because your insurer is committing to pay for the length of your lifetime *or* 20 years.) Alternately, you could receive a "life-only" payout where there is no 20-year guarantee. Here, your payment will be somewhere between $14,000 and $14,500, but if you die early, payments cease and there's nothing more for a beneficiary.

- To determine which is best for you—a 20-year annual payout ($14,000), a 20-year-plus life payment ($12,100), or a life-only payment ($14,500)—seek help from an insurance professional. I myself am a huge believer in incomes that can't be outlived. I tend to favor the 20-year-plus life approach—which can be superior if you have a family—or the life-only annuity if you are very healthy and don't have heirs.

- As I will explain in greater detail in the chapters 3, 6, and 7, annuities may enjoy creditor protection under state laws—during their buildup and payout periods.

I give annuities a 9 out of 10 for their excellence as a retirement income tool. The other advantages with annuities: unlike IRAs, there is no limit on premiums and no requirement to take minimum distributions (RMDs) beginning at age 70½. Payout annuities are a perfect way to distribute income from your core retirement plan.

Scenario B-3: No Tax Deduction with Tax Deferral on Earnings (a Buy-and-Hold Stock Purchase Plan)

Here's a third vehicle that features tax deferral (but does not provide a tax deduction on contributions). It is a "buy-and-hold stock purchase plan"—in which you acquire tax-deferred securities or gold, silver, artwork, coins, or stamps.

In this savings program, $5,000 annually goes where there is nothing but appreciation potential. (Theoretically, this growth stock or asset has no earnings, dividends, or interest.) With 5 percent growth annually, it will be worth $174,000 after 20 years. At that point, this investment will be sold rather than cashed out.

Observations:

- When you sell the assets, you'll pay long-term capital gains taxes of 15 percent—about $11,000—on the $74,000 profit ($174,000 less $100,000). That will leave you with $163,000 in tax-paid retirement income capital. When you turn 65, this cash could acquire a SPIA, where the expected return of $8 per thousand would be $13,000 annually. To figure out what the taxes will be over 20 years, use a $163,000 ÷ $260,000 fraction where about 63 percent ($8,000) of each payment is tax free and 37 percent ($5,000) is taxable.

- During the accumulation phase, there is no creditor protection for the growth asset; a SPIA in the payout phase could offer shelter from claimants.

Taxwise, this is not as good as the annuity strategy in scenario B-2, but it certainly wins out over conventional savings vehicles. I'd give it a 7 on my 1-to-10 scale.

Scenario C: Tax Deduction with Tax-Deferral on Earnings (a Traditional Individual Retirement Account)

Savings vehicles that give a tax deduction on your contributions and tax deferral on your earnings are traditional IRAs and employer-sponsored retirement plans, such as 401(k)s.

Over 90 percent of IRA assets are in tax-deductible, traditional IRAs. It seems that people prefer getting the initial tax deduction on contributions to having their money grow in the tax free environment of a Roth IRA. People also like to roll 401(k) and pension balances into traditional IRAs after they leave a job.

So let's look at what happens when a tax-deductible $5,000 is paid annually into a traditional IRA that builds at 5 percent to $174,000 after 20 years. (Remember that the net annual contribution is only $3,500 because the $5,000 contribution generates $1,500 in tax savings.)

Twenty years hence—at age 65—you could cash out the entire $174,000 and pay taxes on it. Or you could continue to make tax deductible contributions until you are age 70½. At that point, you will have to begin taking RMDs from the account.

When you are age 70½, the RMD will be roughly equivalent to about 4 percent of the account's value on the previous December 31. The percentage will increase gradually to about 8 percent at age 88 (and rapidly thereafter). Here's a puzzler.

Let's say you continue contributions to the account until you are age 70½, at which point you have $250,000. If you merely take out RMDs, allowing what's left in your account to grow at 5 percent annually for another 15 years—when you are age 85—how much will you have then? If you say $250,000, you are correct! (And, somehow if the account could grow at 8 percent, there would be about $400,000 on hand.)

If you are age 45 now, it would be very wise to make that $5,000 annual tax-deductible contribution into a traditional IRA for 25 years, and take *only* RMDs thereafter. You could still end up with $250,000 when you are age 85. Of course, you can always take out more than RMDs, but if you don't need the money, why take it out of a tax-protected, creditor-sheltered environment?

Now that is what I call a good retirement income plan. For me, it rates an 8 on a scale of 1 to 10.

Scenario D-1: No Tax Deduction with Tax Free Earnings (a Cash Value Life Policy Where Loans Are Taken in Retirement)

Now let's look at three savings vehicles that have no tax deductions but do offer a tax free environment for earnings and withdrawals. Each is especially attractive if you believe your tax bracket in retirement will be higher than it is now. One is a cash value life insurance policy where tax free money that has accumulated over 20 years is taken gradually from the policy.

Let's say you pay a $5,000 annual life insurance premium into a level premium life insurance policy for the next 20 years. Before you buy the policy, work carefully with an insurance agent. You'll ask him or her to keep the death benefit low to reduce mortality charges. (I'll assume that this policy has a $246,000 death benefit as I look at a sample policy illustration.) This gives cash values their best chance to increase over the years. During that 20-year period, let's say cash values build up at 5 percent gross interest, before expenses and mortality charges are assessed.

Observations:

- Obviously, this policy emphasizes accumulation and minimizes the death benefit. *Simply put*: The goal is to build up values over 20 years (to age 65) and keep the contract for cash flow in retirement. Keep in mind that if cash values earn about 5 percent interest, there will still be an assessment for expenses and mortality charges. (I'll explain more about these charges in chapters 4 and 5.) Assume that (a) the net buildup will be $145,000 (instead of $174,000), (b) you'll receive $10,000 annually for 20 years, and (c) all payments are tax free. (The distributions don't even count as income when your taxes are calculated on Social Security.)

- Consider that $10,000 tax free is equivalent to a taxable income of $14,300, since you'd have to pay taxes of $4,300—in a 30 percent tax bracket—to leave you with the same $10,000 ($14,300 – $4,300).

- During the accumulation phase, the policy will have its $246,000 death benefit. In the payout phase, the death benefit—after policy loans—will be less, but will pass, free of any income tax obligations, to a beneficiary.

Not bad, when you think about it! In fact, not only will distributions be tax free, they may also be creditor protected, depending on state law. Just be careful to monitor all loan or withdrawal plans. If too much money is distributed for too long, the life policy lapses. Then, all previous distributions are taxed. There is no longer a tax free death benefit either. This is a serious matter to analyze at *least* annually. It helps to obtain policy illustrations for review.

I give this strategy an 8 on a scale of 1 to 10. When you think about retirement income, life insurance is hard to beat. There can be tax-deferred growth, tax free distributions, tax free death benefits, and creditor protection for everyone.

Scenario D-2: No Tax Deduction with Tax Free Earnings (a Life Insurance Death Benefit)

The second vehicle is also life insurance. Here, there are tax free insurance proceeds at an insured's death.

Assume $5,000 goes annually into a level premium, hefty $500,000 life insurance policy. Although there will be some cash value, the emphasis is on inheritance for family instead of retirement income. But, is it really?

Observations:

- If you want to leave something for family, the policy's death benefit accomplishes this neatly. It may permit amortizing or liquidation of other assets that otherwise would produce little if any retirement income.

- Actually, life insurance is the cash that most heirs and inheritors want. In some well-conceived estate plans, insured death benefits are the only thing received. Other assets are spent; the plan is to "die broke," a phrase financial writers Stephen Pollan and Mark Levine put to good use in their 1997 book by the same name (NY: HarperBusiness).

- The tax-free death benefit may even be the source of a beneficiary's income in retirement. (I'll discuss this fully in chapter 10.)

Conclusion: In a die-broke context, life insurance isn't a source of retirement income; instead, a policy makes retirement income from other assets manageable and affordable. I give this strategy a surprising 7 on a 1-to-10 retirement income scale.

Scenario D-3: No Tax Deduction with Tax-Free Earnings (a Municipal Bond Plan)

A tax-free municipal bond (or bond fund) is also a no-tax-deduction savings vehicle that features tax-free earnings.

Let's say a non-deductible $5,000 goes annually into a tax-free muni-bond mutual fund that credits 5 percent interest. You'll have $174,000 in tax-paid money after 20 years. But none of it will be protected from claimants, lawsuits, and bankruptcies.

Let me relate a personal experience. On June 21, 1994, I owned 330.695 shares in a popular muni-bond mutual fund; at $13.57, they were worth $4,487. On June 30, 2008—14 years later—those shares were worth $7,874. Had they earned 5 percent, those shares—14 years later—would have doubled to $9,000. Instead, the rate of growth had been merely 4 percent compounded annually, growing the money from $4,487 to $7,874!

Observations:

- With so much fluctuation in interest rates, it's been difficult to earn 5 percent growth consistently from municipal bond shares.
- Municipal holdings may not have the best bond ratings from rating agencies.
- Municipals cannot be converted into a lifelong income.
- There may be a capital gains tax on profits at liquidation.

Conclusion: I give muni-bond funds a 6 out of 10 as a retirement income plan.

Scenario D-4: No Tax Deduction with Tax-Free Earnings (a Roth Individual Retirement Account or Roth IRA)

Finally, here's the fourth savings vehicle that has no tax deduction, but features tax-free earnings: the Roth IRA. (This option isn't available to everyone; there are income restrictions, as I will explain in chapter 8.)

Let's assume that you make your annual $5,000 contributions into a Roth IRA, which accumulates at 5 percent to $174,000 after 20 years. You had to pay the tax on your earnings before you put the money into a Roth, but once there, the money grows tax free and you can withdraw tax free, as well. This is the consummate example of no tax deduction with tax-free earnings. If you do the math, you'll find the quotient is a nice 34.8.

From a tax standpoint, one of the real advantages of a Roth is that RMDs are *not* required—for you or for your spouse, if you will the account directly to him or her. It is only when the account passes on to loved ones that RMDs must be taken according to a schedule created by the IRS. This makes the Roth IRA perfect—from a tax standpoint—for retirement income and wealth transfer planning.

The other good news—which I will expand on in chapters 3 and 8—is that Roths (and traditional IRAs) offer excellent shelter from creditors, lawsuits, and bankruptcies. As a "no-tax-deduction with tax-free earnings" savings program, there's nothing better. I give Roth IRAs an 8 or 9 on a scale of 1 to 10.

TAX DEDUCTIONS WITH TAX FREE EARNINGS (THE "HOLY GRAIL")

If Congress really wanted to encourage personal retirement income planning, it would approve a "tax deductible with tax free earnings" plan, where you could really come out ahead. (See "Afterword: How We Can All Avert a Retirement Income Crisis," page 221.) Until this happens (possibly by pressure from retirees, or out of necessity), just do the best you can.

As I said earlier, a true "tax deductible with tax free earnings" retirement income planning strategy doesn't exist. Roths and traditional IRAs each give one element, but not the other. Most 401(k)s and pensions are similar to traditional IRAs; they offer tax deductions and tax deferral during accumulation. Only Roth arrangements assure distributions that are tax free.

I can think of only two legitimate "tax deductible into tax free schemes," but they work for the beneficiary—not the benefactor—and involve life insurance. First, there are employer group term insurance plans where premiums for a $50,000 tax free death benefit are tax deductible (and there are no cash values). Second, there is life insurance in an employer's traditional pension plan where premiums become deductible; then (after a small employee tax cost), an insurance benefit is tax free at death.

When it comes to pure income planning, however, it's presently impossible to contribute "tax deductible with tax free earnings." You just can't get $5,000 (which only costs you $3,500 net) into a tax free savings program with a 20th year tax free yield of $174,000 (at 5 percent) and a quotient of 49.7.

In conclusion, the tax savings afforded by life insurance, annuities, IRAs, qualified plans, and growth assets make them the obvious choice when planning for retirement income. This is true whether you can earn 5, 6, 8, or 10 percent, or even higher rates of return. Simply put, if you focus on these savings vehicles for core income, you won't need an investment guru; you'll be doing just fine.

PROTECT YOUR SAVINGS
FROM CLAIMANTS

I finally know what separates man from beasts:
financial worries.
—*Jules Renard*

You can be disciplined in your spending, smart about saving and investing, and an excellent steward of your money. And then the unexpected occurs: you get into a car accident, someone trips on the walkway to your office, or a patient you treated once while her doctor was away names you as a party in a malpractice suit that has nothing to do with the condition for which you treated her. Perhaps someone decides you have so much wealth that they deserve a share too. Maybe that's what entered the mind of Allen Heckard in 2006 when he sued Michael Jordan and Nike Founder Phil Knight for $832 million dollars, claiming emotional distress and defamation because people often mistook him for the basketball star. Fortunately for all concerned, Heckard dropped the lawsuit later that same year.

Crazier things have happened. That's why interest in asset protection planning is on the rise. The field is relatively new; it began as a stand-alone area of the law in the 1970s but didn't begin gaining ground until the 1990s. Asset protection planning concerns itself with a set of legal techniques and a body of statutory and common law meant to protect individuals and businesses from civil judgments.

In this chapter (and in more detailed and specific asset protection sections in upcoming chapters), we'll look at how to safeguard your retirement income now, before anyone tries to claim it. (I'll refer to such individuals as "claimants" because—as you can see from the previous example—not everyone is a legitimate creditor.)

Ideally, as a good steward of your money, you'll shelter all retirement income structures from claimants and lawsuits—even bankruptcy filings. Please don't misunderstand me. I am *not* telling you to skirt the law. Never—and I repeat—*never* hide your assets or do something reckless or illegal to mislead creditors. Rather, make legitimate use of asset protection law and take the proper steps before there's even a whiff of trouble. Otherwise, it may be too late. Attempts to shelter your assets when there's a claimant at the ready may be rightly interpreted as trying to hinder, delay, or defraud creditors.

Asset protection planning to guard against a future bankruptcy filing seems especially important. At the end of this chapter in Asset Protection Resources, I refer to a 2009 article in the *Harvard Law & Policy Revue*. It shows that the relative share of bankruptcy filings among mature individuals increased significantly from 1991 to 2007—even as it *decreased* for people under age 55. In 1991, just 21,465 individuals aged 65 to 74 filed for bankruptcy. This was just 1.8 percent of all those declaring bankruptcy. In 2007, 57,623 seniors filed. This accounted for 5 percent of all those declaring bankruptcy—a 177.8 percent increase!

If you drill down further, the numbers tell an even more alarming story. During that 16-year period, the rate of bankruptcy rose by 150.8 percent for individuals ages 55 to 64 and by a whopping 566.7 percent for individuals ages 75 and older. With life expectancies increasing and the 2008–2009 stock market meltdown, this isn't a good trend for seniors going forward.

THE BASICS

To safeguard personal assets, financial planners recommend umbrella or personal liability insurance. They also form family businesses (corporations, limited liability companies, and family limited partnerships) and, where appropriate, trusts in debtor-friendly countries to protect personal investments. Foreign trusts are considered useful because some nine out of ten lawsuits in the world are filed in the United States, the most creditor-friendly country in the world. In the United States, it seems that anyone can throw a lawsuit, frivolous or not, at the system. Conversely, most foreign countries are debtor friendly and frown on civil lawsuits. They don't give contingent lawyers' fees. Plaintiffs post bonds (and pay all legal fees if they lose the case). In a few of these countries, it's almost impossible to file claims in court. (That's why asset protection lawyers suggest locating assets in offshore trusts.)

Liability insurance and the business structures I mentioned earlier aren't the only way to protect savings and investments from others who want them. Having carefully studied creditor exemptions in the law, I have come to this conclusion: Exempt property seems to be increasing in significance. Realize, however, that legislators can remove, lessen, or modify these statutes at any time.

HOW THE FOUR KEY SAVINGS INSTRUMENTS "OUTSHINE" CONVENTIONAL SAVINGS AND INVESTMENTS

What should you do to protect the money you've set aside for retirement? My recommendation: Get that serious cash into life insurance, annuities, IRAs/QPs, and your home. Why? Because each can be uniquely safeguarded from future claimants, lawsuits, and bankruptcy.

You won't find that kind of protection with conventional savings instruments and investments. In fact, I challenge you to read the law on conventional savings vehicles and investments to see if you can find anything about asset protection features. You won't. You won't find buffers for CDs, money markets, treasuries, stocks, investment real estate, art, coins, stamps, or even gold. Claimants don't have any trouble putting a lien on these assets. Occasionally, you'll find old-time laws that exempt six cows, an ox, and a tractor, but even these are unlikely nowadays.

In short, don't look for creditor protective exclusions and exemptions in the law when you acquire a conventional investment because you won't find them. *Don't get me wrong*—certainly, there are good reasons to buy personally owned CDs, treasuries, stocks, bonds, and mutual funds. But if you want protection from personal claimants, lawsuits, and bankruptcy, put your money in life insurance, annuities, IRAs/QPs, and your home. That's key, if you want to protect yourself from the unexpected—and unpleasant—surprises.

CLAIMANT PROTECTION FOR THE FOUR KEY SAVINGS VEHICLES

In the upcoming chapters on life insurance, annuities, IRAs, and home ownership, you will find detailed information on the asset protection safeguards in place for each—and the limits on them. In Appendix A section A, you will find a chart summarizing how much protection—or how little—each state provides for life insurance cash values and annuities. The chart covers cash values and death proceeds for annuities, but cash values *only* for life insurance policies.

Here I will just sketch out the basics.

Life Insurance

Generally speaking, most states give life insurance policies significant creditor protection to encourage a base of coverage. This is to motivate people to do right by their families so the burden of support does not fall on society should the breadwinner die. Virtually all states give at least partial protection to cash values in personally owned life insurance policies. When it comes to death proceeds, however, things become a bit more complicated. Typically, a state's creditor exemption is available *only* if that beneficiary is an actual person or a trust. In other words, in most states, proceeds of insurance paid to "my estate" aren't sheltered from anyone's creditors.

Consider also that about 35 states have specific laws that make it clear that insurance premiums paid to hinder, delay, or defraud creditors aren't safeguarded from anyone's creditors. While that is not true of all states, assume that the system frowns on attempts to hide money from anyone.

Annuities

These are at least partially protected in about two-thirds of the states, but they don't enjoy the same level of safeguards as life insurance. That's because people don't tend to buy annuities to provide family support after the death of a breadwinner.

However, a number of states do shelter annuity cash values and death proceeds. Some 17 provide complete or nearly complete protection for cash values and death proceeds; another 19 offer partial protection. The rest offer little if any safeguards.

And as with life insurance, you can't pay annuity premiums to hinder, delay, or defraud creditors. That said, you will still want to acquaint yourself with the laws in your state regarding both. If state law affords more shelter for insurance than annuities, and such shelter is a priority for you, it is prudent to make life insurance the key component in your retirement income plan. And if you live in a state where the law affords little protection, you may want to retire in a state like Florida or Texas that affords more protection. (I'll discuss the specific laws later in chapters on life insurance, annuities, IRAs, and home ownership.)

IRAs/QPs

When it comes to asset protection, you probably can't do any better than IRAs and qualified plans (QPs)—pensions, 401(k)s, etc. Because of that, you should keep these accounts intact. If you have to borrow money, exhaust all other possibilities before tapping any of these savings plans. If you're the beneficiary of IRA/QP funds, keep good records that trace where the inherited IRA came from.

In bankruptcy, all assets in QPs are *fully* exempt from most creditor claims. When your IRA funds come from QPs to IRAs, they have the full exemption given QPs. But you should separate these IRA rollovers from tax deductible annual contribution accounts. The reason is that the latter are protected only up to $1 million, as adjusted for inflation.

Outside of bankruptcy, funds in most QPs are fully shielded under federal law—thanks to the Employee Retirement Income

Security Act of 1974 (ERISA). IRAs are shielded under state laws only; 42 states give full protection for traditional IRAs, 36 for Roth IRAs.

Personal Residences

All 50 states have "homestead" exemptions that protect personal residences from creditors and in bankruptcy. These exemptions refer to equity in a primary residence and are meant to prevent forced sales of homes to meet demands of creditors. The exemptions shelter is normally automatic; however, a homeowner must some-times file for protection. Forced sales that simply satisfy mortgages, mechanics liens, or property taxes are not exempt. In most states, homestead exemptions (from $5,000 to $100,000) are relatively low, but they are rising. However, a dozen states have high limits (or virtually no limits). And Florida's liberal law may even protect sales proceeds put in a bank account as long as the homeowner has a genuine intent to purchase another home in Florida.

—

With each of these savings vehicles, the trick is to keep withdrawals, distributions, rollovers/transfers, and inherited accounts protected too. Ask your lawyer about protection for payouts from insurance policies, annuities, and IRA/QPs, and inherited accounts that pass under beneficiary forms. In general creditor situations, look to state laws and research the Bankruptcy Abuse Prevention and Consumer Protection Act of 2005 (BAPA) regarding bankruptcies. Then build a retirement income strategy using creditor exemptions in the law. It could come in handy someday.

I also recommend visiting the local law library and making friends with the librarians. Do your homework and learn how the laws in your state could protect your retirement income from others. Review everything carefully with your planning team. Take advantage of every system safeguard! In uncertain times, your money depends on it.

WILL O.J. SIMPSON KEEP HIS ASSETS?

You are probably familiar with Fred Goldman's successful civil lawsuit in 1997 against O.J. Simpson. Since then, Mr. Simpson has vigorously avoided paying Mr. Goldman the money the court awarded him. This situation is worth studying if you are interested in learning more about the ins and outs of safeguarding your assets from creditors. Here is my analysis, based solely on press reports involving their disputes.

In 1997, a court reportedly awarded the estates of Ron Goldman (nearly $20 million) and Nicole Brown Simpson ($13.5 million) in a civil lawsuit against O.J. Simpson. Mr. Goldman has pressed for payment; Mr. Simpson has resisted.

Seemingly, O.J. Simpson is living off income from a $4 million NFL pension fund. This fund and payments from it are protected from creditors. Mr. Simpson owns a $1 million home also, sheltered fully under Florida's unlimited homestead exemption. In other words, he is legitimately taking advantage of system safeguards outlined in this chapter. Mr. Goldman can't do much about it.

In 2008, however, O.J. Simpson was sentenced to 33 years in prison—without the possibility of parole for 9 years. He is currently serving that sentence at the Lovelock Correctional Institute in Lovelock, Nevada. Let's look at how this might change things, from a creditor protection perspective:

1. O.J. Simpson now "resides" in Nevada, not Florida. He may be there a long time. Is this considered a change of residence, for planning purposes?

2. If so, Nevada's limited homestead exemption seemingly substitutes for Florida's unlimited exemption. If that's the case, any excess becomes available to O.J. Simpson's creditors.

3. It appears that O.J. Simpson's $4 million protected NFL pension fund generates $20,000 to $25,000 in monthly income. Under Florida law, this payment should be safeguarded—even on receipt. If Nevada law is less protective, can his creditors attach these payments wherever deployed? (Know that he probably won't need much of that money in prison for support.)

4. Finally, let's say O.J. Simpson has rolled over some of his pension to an IRA. If so, it seems that Nevada is less protective than Florida. And his creditors should take note.

To sum up, it appears that O.J. Simpson has enjoyed many creditor system safeguards during his stay in Florida—at least until now. Since he is currently a Nevada resident, it could be Fred Goldman's time to benefit from the system.

Time will tell!

WORKING WITH YOUR ATTORNEY IF YOU GET INTO A JAM WITH CREDITORS

Let's get one thing very clear: It is *not* my intention to help anyone skirt the law. But unexpected things happen. That's why I urge you to study the asset protection basics in this book now, while your financial situation is stable. Work with your financial and legal advisors to implement the strategies most appropriate for your situation and location. Knowing you have legal protection in place will help you sleep better at night.

Depending on your means, your asset-protection plan might be the equivalent of a finely tuned Mercedes; in other words, a family limited partnership and an offshore trust. Or, it could be a more basic Mazda-style program with plenty of simple system safeguards—some combination of cash value life insurance, annuities, IRAs/QPs, and home equity, since these frequently have asset protection features that other savings plans don't offer. Just don't settle for the asset-protection equivalent of an Edsel.

Let's take a moment to look into the future—one that I hope you never face. I am taking you here because I want to share the steps you should take to help limit the damage if you do meet with a crisis. Let's start off on a good note: we'll imagine that you were prudent when life was calmer, and you took the time to stash a fair amount of your cash into the asset-protected savings vehicles I've recommended. Now, however, something ominous is looming. It's serious—it could be a potential claim arising from a car accident or a fire on your property in which someone was injured—and the finger of blame is pointing at you. At this moment, it also looks as if your umbrella or personal liability insurance policy is ineffective or insufficient. Now what?

Here's what I recommend when you meet with your attorney:

A. Do your homework, research your best options, and be prepared to take the lead in the discussion. Know that many quality lawyers are good at "putting out fires"; they aren't always schooled in how to avoid problems. You need to help them.

B. As part of your research, do a Google search pairing "asset protection" with each of the following terms: "life insurance," "annuities," "tax-qualified retirement plans," "IRAs," "home equity" and "investments." Print copies of the best results, including court cases and statutory law. Prepare a file for your lawyer.

C. Soak up the law as if you were researching your medical options after being diagnosed with cancer. Your financial well-being may be as important as good mental or physical health, and it is likely to affect both.

Here are eight questions you should ask an attorney, where communication is privileged and private. Let's imagine that a claim is pending; it has gone beyond the "threat" phase. Make it your goal to help your lawyer become familiar with all possibilities as you see them, recognizing of course that you can't build a case to hide assets from your creditors.

The answers here may seem obvious—either yes or no. However, the laws may vary greatly from state to state, so don't make any assumptions. Seek out a lawyer who can advise you on the best moves in your state, and consider his or her counsel carefully.

1. "Should I take out a second mortgage to reduce my home's equity to the homestead exemption amount?" Alternately: "Should I make advance payments on the mortgage to increase home *equity* to the exemption level?"

2. "Should I borrow cash values from my life insurance and acquire a simple premium immediate annuity (SPIA), if that gives more protection? The SPIA will pay me a lifetime income and include a spendthrift clause."

3. "Should I incorporate my business activities—or form a limited liability company (LLC), if that helps? The business might establish a tax-qualified retirement pension plan with a mandatory contribution on my behalf and that of my employees."

4. "Should I leave any required minimum distributions in my QP and IRA?" (Required minimum distributions are amounts of money you are required to withdraw from a QP or IRA at age 70½.) I don't advise doing this; you'll have to pay a 50 percent penalty tax on any shortfalls.

5. "Should I annuitize my IRA into a support income stream for myself and my dependents?"

6. "Should I move to a state like Florida or Texas to obtain better creditor protection for my retirement income cornerstones? If so, is there a time limit before I must go?"

7. "Should I convert my accumulation annuity to a payout program and direct all payments to a family support checking account?"

8. "If I am entitled to extra earned income over the upcoming months, would it help to defer that to a later date?"

Again, my goal is to make your conversations fruitful. I am *not* advocating that you hide anything from creditors or make a preferential transfer in bankruptcy. If you get into trouble, you'll need the best advice on how to manage your insurance/annuity policies, QPs/IRAs, home equity, and personal checking accounts that are already in place.

Your goal should be to do everything legitimately possible to protect assets (and the retirement income they provide) from others who may want them. This includes helping your lawyer become as well informed as you are about practical solutions! Once he or she knows what you are considering, you can work together to determine your best course of action and swiftly implement it.

ASSET PROTECTION RESOURCES

If you are interested in serious asset protection, let me suggest the publications of Barry Engel, a friend and a widely recognized asset protection attorney and authority. His writings are compelling and understandable. Indeed, he views safeguarding as a way of life. As he has said on more than one occasion, "If you look over your shoulder to see who's after your money, you aren't paranoid. These people are really there." Start with his *Asset Protection Planning Guide,* second ed. (Commerce Clearing House, 2005). It is very informative.

Engel, by the way, is credited with the introduction and development of the offshore trust concept. He is also known for the development of asset protection trust law statutes in the Cook Islands.

If you are interested in "stretch" IRAs, IRA distributions, and creditor protection for accounts, I strongly recommend the writings of Edwin P. Morrow III, J.D., LL.M, RFC, principal, Morrow Law Offices. In 2007, Mr. Morrow wrote or coauthored three excellent articles in *Journal of Retirement Planning.* You can order the journal from Commerce Clearing House (CCH), 1-800-449-8114, www.CCHGroup.com. You can also find current articles on Mr. Morrow's web site: http://www.morrowlaw.com/our_services.

Finally, if you are interested in the topic of senior citizens and bankruptcy, I recommend reading "The Increasing Vulnerability of Older Americans: Evidence from Bankruptcy Court," by Deborah Thome, Elizabeth Warren, and Teresa Sullivan. The article ran in the *Harvard Law & Policy Review,* Volume 3, Number 1 (2009). It is available at http://www.hlpronline.com.

Part 2

INCREASE YOUR RETIREMENT INCOME

CASH VALUE LIFE INSURANCE: THE BASICS

---

*A man is rich in proportion to the things
he can afford to let alone.*
—*Henry David Thoreau*

The first savings instrument I want you to consider for your rock-solid retirement plan is cash value life insurance. This is a type of life insurance that not only pays death benefits but, as you might have guessed, also allows you to build savings that grow tax deferred over time. These savings take the form of cash values—a reserve— which earn "interest" and eventually endow the policy, usually at an insured's age 100. Interest rates will be competitive—in 2010, as high as 4 or 5 percent. Once the policy accumulates enough cash value, you can use it to withdraw a monthly retirement income, or take out tax-free loans against the account.

For example, imagine you are age 60 and you've been paying annual premiums of $20,000 into a $1 million insurance policy for 20 years or so. By this point, cash values will have accumulated enough for you to withdraw, say, $30,000 a year, for a number of years, depending on the policy. You need to take care, however, that you don't take out so much money that the policy collapses. (A policy will basically collapse if withdrawals and loans exceed cash value and no more money is put in.)

I like cash value policies as the first essential in a retirement income plan because they meet my criteria: First, they offer a safe place to stash serious money. Insurance is a highly regulated industry. Second, as I touched on in chapter 3, cash value life insurance can afford a certain measure of asset protection. Some state laws protect policy cash values from personal creditors, which means that no one can seize the money while it is in your policy. (See "Appendix A: A State-by-State Look at How the Law Safeguards Life Insurance Cash Values and Annuity Cash Values and Death Proceeds," starting on page 229.) Normally, state laws safeguard the money as it passes from your policy to your heirs. Depending on the state in which you live, the money may be safe from when you pay the insurance premiums to the time your heirs spend it.

Third, cash value life insurance confers certain tax advantages that other savings vehicles don't. If you invest in a certificate of deposit (CD), for instance, you'll pay tax on earnings each year. But you won't have to pay taxes on interest or other earnings credited to cash value until you withdraw your profits from the policy. And with one exception (Modified Endowment Contracts, which I will spell out later), you won't pay taxes if you borrow cash that has accumulated in the policy. Finally, in almost all cases, your beneficiaries won't pay income tax on the proceeds. That adds up to a lot of tax savings!

Here are still other advantages:

- If you are a highly compensated executive who has maxed out on your IRA or 401(k) contribution, know that there are no contribution limits when buying cash value life insurance.

- There is no distribution requirement at age 70½.

- Unlike IRAs and accumulation annuities, income taken from life insurance before age 59½ is generally not subject to tax penalties.

- Don't forget the death benefit. Over the years, I've found that beneficiaries like to receive cash (which they can certainly use for an income in retirement). They'll always prefer some tax-free insurance money to an asset that's hard to sell.

The ideal time to buy one or more of these policies is when you first begin to pull together the components of your retirement plan. For many of you, that's likely to be when you're in your 40s. Keep in mind that you'll need to allow sufficient time for your policy to acquire cash value before you can make withdrawals without being penalized for it. Since initial premiums are typically used to cover costs associated with selling the contract (a "front-end" charge), the amount available may be significantly lower than the sum of premiums paid—or even zero—for some time. Consequently, cash value grows slowly in the beginning. Later, interest credited will compensate for that initial loss. That's when the earnings pick up speed.

UNDERSTANDING THE VARIABLES: INTEREST CREDITS, EXPENSES, AND MORTALITY COSTS

Life insurance, though simple in concept, is *not* so simple in practice. What you pay in premiums—and what you ultimately get for your money (in cash values and death benefits)—depends on factors such as interest credits, expense charges, and mortality costs.

Let me help you become conversant with all of these by explaining how a premium is determined.

Let's assume you're 40 and considering a Universal Life insurance policy that will pay a $100,000 death benefit. (Although there are other kinds of cash value policies, Universal Life is great for illustration purposes here because it offers flexibility in calculating premiums, cash values, and death benefits. These popular policies began in the 1970s and are quite sensitive to changes in interest rates, expense charges, and mortality costs.)

Let's also assume that your life expectancy is age 80. That means—from the insurance carrier's perspective—that you will probably pay premiums for at least another 40 years. Given that, how much will the insurer charge you per year to cover the cost of the $100,000 death benefit? Some might figure $2,500 ($100,000 ÷ 40). That's a logical guess—but fortunately, it's too high.

You'll pay less. In fact, your insurer will *discount* your premium (in advance) based on the fact that what you pay in will earn interest. This is the interest "credited" to your policy's cash value, or your "reserve." (As I write this in 2010, 4 or 5 percent seems like a reasonable long-term interest rate, so your $2,500 annual premium might drop down to about $800.)

Next, the insurance company will charge for annual expenses and mortality costs—based on your chances of dying each year, according to actuarial tables. These charges are usually converted to a level amount, say, $200 annually for your policy. If so, your premium becomes $1,000 ($800 plus $200).

It's as simple as that.

A word of caution: You'll want to read a sample policy carefully and determine how interest credits, expenses, and mortality costs are computed for your contract with an insurer. In some cases, these items are guaranteed, meaning they can't be changed by the insurer, no matter what happens. In other instances, these can be modified and changed. As a general rule, if these items are guaranteed, premiums are higher. This can be worth the additional expense.

Over a period of years, changes in interest rates in an interest-sensitive policy—usually Universal Life contracts—can have a significant effect on premiums. For instance, in the late 70s and early 80s, interest rate credits were very high—in the double digits. If someone acquired that Universal Life policy in 1980, his or her first premium would have been much lower—from $1,000 down to perhaps $500. Since then, interest rates have gradually decreased and—at the time this book went to press—were in the 1 to 5 percent range for money markets, CDs, and treasuries. If policyowners hadn't *increased* their premiums as interest credits *decreased* between 1980 and today, their policy would have been seriously "underfunded" now. It may even have lapsed or nearly lapsed.

Given how interest ranges have dropped over a 30-year period, you should closely review with a life insurance agent any interest-sensitive life insurance policy that you may have. Ask for contract illustrations that are based on various annual inputs. You may need to increase your premiums to avoid a policy cancellation for lack of cash values.

Finally, say you pay in $1,000 annually for your $100,000 policy. Everything goes well with interest credits, expenses, and mortality costs. Your policy moves along as expected. Here is a rough snapshot of how things might look going forward.

Accumulation of Value in a $100,000 Universal Life Policy

Year	After Annual Premiums of $1,000	Cash Values	Death Benefit
10	$10,000	$6,000	$100,000
20	$20,000	$20,000	$100,000
40	$40,000	$60,000	$100,000
60	$60,000	$100,000*	$100,000

*At age 100, your policy endows, and if you are still alive, you receive the $100,000 death benefit in the form of cash values.

A STORY ILLUSTRATION

At this point, you may be asking yourself, "Why would I want to sink serious money into an insurance policy? Can't I do better investing it on my own?"

Again, that depends on your priorities. As I said in the first chapter, the four savings vehicles I recommend give you the best chance to have retirement income you can count on when you need it. This straightforward comparison of two financial propositions may help you appreciate the advantages life insurance offers over other savings vehicles.

Let's say the first proposition comes to you from your friend, Tom. He proposes that you pay him $4,000 each year until you die. Then, he'll give your family $500,000. Since Tom is pretty good with money, he just might pull this off. You run the numbers. You are age 40 now. If you die at age 80, a $500,000 payoff to your family will amount to a 5 percent rate of return compounded annually on payments of $4,000. Not bad! Of course, the return would be "enormous" if you die early, say in 20 years or so.

Later, at a dinner meeting with your banker, Harry, you explain Tom's plan.

"Are you crazy?" Harry is aghast. "First off, it could be a gambling contract and illegal in this state. Second, what happens if you miss a payment? And any earnings on your money are surely taxable, even if they temporarily belong to Tom. Who watches Tom? If he skips town, dies, or goes bankrupt, what happens then? Further, you are healthy and might live 50 or even 60 years; don't pay into something that loses money the longer you live. I wouldn't like the deal even if he were to give you 10 percent and cut the payments in half!"

Harry refers you to Dan, who heads the bank's insurance department. You meet with him the next day. Dan explains why a life insurance policy that requires a $5,000 payment each year—it's called a "premium"—can give you a much better deal than the one Tom is offering you.

Let's call the insurance company "ABC Co." Dan says that ABC can offer you a "flexible" or "universal" life insurance policy. If you die 40 years later at age 80, the payout to your family would be the same $500,000 Tom promised. That would amount to a 4 percent rate of return compounded annually on your premiums. You listen politely, but you're still not sold. Why would you want to pay $1,000 more a year to get that same $500,000 death benefit?

But then Dan says a few things that get your attention. He assures you that ABC Co. has a good rating with A.M. Best, Standard & Poor's, Fitch, and Moody's. Such *rating agencies* give consumer reports on carrier strength, credit worthiness, and capacity to handle risk. Odds are, he says, that ABC Co. will be in business when it's time to pay up. Can you be sure that Tom will still be around?

Second, there are safeguards in the insurance system to protect you and your policy in the event that a company as solid as ABC fails. *Insurance departments* monitor insurance company marketing practices, Dan explains. If an insurer fails, *guaranty associations* assess other carriers to pay any lost benefits. *Other carriers* stand ready to take over failed insurers. You have none of these safeguards with Tom's proposition. (Note: Given recent events regarding the financial services industry, you've surely heard that some insurers have been given lower scores by the rating agencies. I wouldn't worry much about your carrier. The insurance industry is too important to fail. I will explain more about this in chapter 6.)

Third, as I said earlier, the cash values and payout to beneficiaries may be safe from creditors, depending on the laws in your state.

The other key advantage: ABC's policy is life insurance—and that means you won't pay income tax on the face amount someday, or on interest earned on the premiums. With Tom's proposition, you'd have to pay taxes on any earnings.

Finally, policy values could pay an income in retirement—something that Tom is not promising.

In summary, ABC's real $500,000 policy costs $5,000 annually. If you die at age 80, you'll pay $200,000 in premiums over the 40 years. The beneficiary will get $500,000—$300,000 of which is tax-free "interest" (that's 4 percent compounded annually on the premiums). During that entire time, the money in the policy will be shielded from taxes and, presumably, everyone's creditors. Tom's proposal can't compete with that.

Still, you're skeptical. "Isn't ABC promising more than it can deliver?"

Dan assures you that ABC can deliver. He explains:

1. ABC invests lots of money each day, mostly in bonds and mortgages. Because of that, it should earn more on your money than you or Tom can. Surely millions attract better rates than a few thousand dollars. ABC credits all net interest earnings to the policy's cash values. Then, ABC charges its expenses to the policy. Since there will also be death claims regularly, ABC assesses for everyone's share of its mortality costs.

2. You could say that a life policy has a cash value "account" where interest is earned and expenses and mortality costs are levied. ABC is entitled to a profit, and it charges for this too. While it's a little more complicated than that, that's the general idea. Of course, policyholders are entirely dependent on the general account of ABC, which is for the benefit of all creditors of the company. (This is for so-called *fixed* or guaranteed cost policies. If you invest in *variable* policies, whose cash values depend on fluctuations in mutual funds,

most premium dollars are placed in separate accounts that generally aren't subject to claims against the insurer.)

3. Here's another reason these accounts can accumulate money more quickly than you could if you invested that money as an individual. Some policyowners won't pay premiums, and they'll surrender or lapse their policies. The good news here is that ABC may already have charged for a share of death claims on the cancelled policies. Since you'll be keeping your policy, you could receive extra interest credits or dividends for your share of any savings.

4. It's obvious that a beneficiary gets a death benefit someday. However, the policyowner can use the account while alive, provided he or she is knowledgeable about policy management. (I'll discuss the ins and outs a little later on in this chapter.)

Is there a downside? As long as you keep the policy in force, not much! If you die later in life and pay in more, the return will be less. That's the trade-off for living a longer life and beating the odds. If you die younger than expected, however, without contributing as much in premiums, your heirs will still get the $500,000, possibly a windfall. "Some people," says Dan, "spend other assets to zero before 'dying broke' but leave life insurance intact for the family."

CASH VALUE LIFE INSURANCE: THE PERFECT INVESTMENT

When you think about it, level premium cash value insurance offers almost everything you'd want in a blueprint for sound financial planning. It's only when you buy too much and cancel too soon that these policies don't work. Otherwise, it can work very well. Let me give you some examples.

Take Charlie, who chooses minimum coverage and maximum cash value accumulation. When he reaches retirement, he smartly takes withdrawals and earns a steady 4 to 5 percent geometric rate of return over the years.

Then there's John, who acquires maximum coverage with minimum cash value. He keeps paying premiums until death and earns a robust 5 or 6 percent geometric tax-free rate of return for his family.

Finally, there's Malcolm Forbes. In December 1989, the *Los Angeles Times* reported that much of the income of Forbes, Inc., was used to purchase enormous amounts of estate tax-free life insurance on his life. Two months later, *The New York Times* reported that Malcolm's son, Steve Forbes, assumed control of the company to fulfill his father's wish that Forbes, Inc., remain a family business. One week later, *The New York Times* reported that Malcolm Forbes had died.

I'm told that Mr. Forbes was insured for well over $100 million, most of which was acquired within a year or two of his death. The important thing, however, is that he had the foresight to deal with his own mortality and take steps to perpetuate *Forbes* magazine for all of us. Indeed!

SOME BASIC FACTS ABOUT CASH VALUE LIFE INSURANCE

Dan has just given a very simple explanation of how life insurance works. In truth, however, life insurance policies can have many moving parts. There are also many types of life insurance policies and large price differences among companies offering identical coverage. In addition, with cash value life insurance policies, the size of the cash value buildup can differ substantially from company to company, and there is sometimes no correlation between the size of the cash value and premiums paid. In short, it can get very complicated. That's why it's critical to find the most knowledgeable insurance agent you can. (Please see "Choosing an Insurance Agent and Insurance Company," next.)

CHOOSING AN INSURANCE AGENT AND INSURANCE COMPANY

The best way to find a good insurance agent is to ask family members, friends, and business associates for referrals. Then take the time to interview a few candidates. I recommend those who have additional education, such as CLUs (Chartered Life Underwriters), ChFCs (Chartered Financial Consultants), and CFPs (Certified Financial Planners). There are other quality designations as well.

Both CLUs and CFPs have taken special courses in financial planning, economics, finance, fringe benefits, annuities, life insurance, pensions, and estate planning. A CFP focuses a bit more on investments, while CLUs are more insurance oriented and spend more time on insurance and actuarial studies. The courses are roughly equivalent to an extra year in college. Both CLUs and CFPs can be licensed to sell almost anything. They may be licensed with the state insurance department and with the SEC (Securities and Exchange Commission) if they sell securities.

When you interview agents, ask them to tell you about their additional education and their state licenses and have them show you the documents to prove it.

In addition, they should have licenses with one or more insurance carriers that have a good rating with A.M. Best, Fitch, Moody's, and Standard & Poor's, agencies that assign safety ratings to insurance companies.

Finally, make sure the insurance companies these agents represent are ones that:

1. Collectively provide a menu of insurance options: *Whole Life* (fully guaranteed; it may also give dividends declared by the insurer); *Universal Life* (lower premiums and less guaranteed); *Indexed Life* (where interest credits can improve if market indexes— Dow Jones, Standard & Poor's, NASDAQ, etc.— perform well); *Term or Temporary Life* (where there are no cash values); and *Variable Life* (where policy values reflect fluctuations in mutual funds).

2. Treat all policyholders fairly. For example, insurers have only a certain amount of interest for their policies, old and new. I like strong insurers that first credit competitive rates to existing policies. (I define what I mean by "competitive" in chapter 6 on annuities.)

To get back to basics, there are two kinds of life insurance: term life and permanent. If you buy term life insurance, you'll receive life insurance coverage for a specific period—say 5, 10, 15, 20, or 30 years. If you live past the "term" you have chosen, your beneficiaries won't receive a payout. Term life insurance does not accumulate cash values. In the early years, it is less expensive than permanent life insurance, and generally advisable for individuals in their 20s and 30s who are starting their careers.

Permanent life insurance—which covers you for your entire life-time—dedicates a portion of your level premium payment toward a cash value account that grows tax deferred over time. You actually "overpay" in the early years so you won't have to pay so much later on when you are likely to have less income. The overpayment creates a reserve, which is the cash value. The cash value in your policy grows each year with interest tax deferred. As interest is credited to the account, the value builds continuously. Thanks to the growing reserve, the assessed cost of the life insurance could even decline.

The "face amount" of life insurance is the initial amount for which you apply. If you buy a $500,000 policy, for instance, the face amount is $500,000. The insurance company applies a mortality cost to the face amount, minus the reserve (as defined earlier). The less the net difference, the more the cash value builds. The cash value is designed to grow so that it equals the face value (and endows), usually when the insured individual reaches age 100.

Cash value life insurance doesn't actually become *permanently yours* until 2 years from the date of purchase. Until then, the insurance company has the right to cancel the policy if it finds an error in the policy application process. (If it can prove fraud, however, it can cancel at any time.) After the 2 years have passed, you can cancel the policy but the insurance company can't, even if your health suddenly deteriorates. In Colorado, insurers have to pay death benefits even if the insured commits suicide one year and a day after buying the policy. (I've actually had two friends who took out policies and committed suicide on that first day of the 2nd year.)

There are also limits on who you can take out a policy on. You can buy insurance on yourself, of course, and anyone else in whom you have an "insurable interest" at the time you buy the policy. In other words, a policyowner must stand to gain from continuance of life—or lose emotionally or financially by someone's death. Parents, spouses, and children have blood or marriage ties—and insurable interests in each other. By affinity, there are insurable interests in relatives and in-laws, or if financial support could be lost at death. Creditors have insurable interests in debtors (to the extent of debts and life premiums on the debtor's life), and business owners can insure each other and key employees (to the extent of a potential loss). At present—at least, as this book was written—the insurance industry does not recognize direct insurable interest for same-sex partners, charities that insure donors, or corporations that insure rank and file employees. These areas of the law are still being sorted out.

However, once the policy is yours, there is nothing to stop you from naming *anyone* as your beneficiary—unless you live in Kentucky or Texas, where the law dictates that the only beneficiaries you can name are those individuals who stand to lose financially at the insured's death. There is also nothing to stop you, the policyowner, from gifting or selling the policy to a new owner, who need not have an insurable interest in your life. There's no problem with this if you're the one doing the selling or switching the beneficiary, but consider the possible consequences if someone who receives your policy sells it to someone who would suffer no financial loss if you died, but would profit from the death benefits. (See "Bad Insurance Practices," next.)

BAD INSURANCE PRACTICES

In the 18th century, you could take out life policies on strangers for speculative purposes. For obvious reasons, this "wagering" practice is now void and against public policy, as it should be. But mischief continues. Remember that a policyowner can transfer the policy to a new owner who needn't have an insurable interest in the insured. That means, for instance, that a business partner could take out a policy on you, then sell the policy to a soldier of fortune. And there probably isn't a thing you can do about it.

It is also possible to buy Stranger Owned Life Insurance (STOLI). Here's a brief explanation of how it works:

An insurance agent advises you to "apply for a large policy on your life," perhaps one with a face amount large enough to equal your net worth. A friendly lender will pay premiums for at least 2 years (until the policy's incontestable period expires). There is even better news. You aren't personally responsible for these nonrecourse loans. After 2 years, a buyer, a STOLI purchaser, will surface, acquire the policy, pay off your loan and put real money in your pocket. In other words, you purchase a policy you never dreamed of buying. Later, after "renting" your insurance for 2 years, you sell it, and step out gracefully with a profit.

Here's the problem. It's understood that individuals have an unlimited insurable interest in their own life. (Surely not everyone wants to commit suicide.) So, carriers will issue a large amount of personal insurance to someone who is also the insured.

Talk about tempting fate! If there is a STOLI transaction, and the worst happens, could your family sue the carrier for issuing "too much" insurance? If so, you won't be around to enjoy the victory.

The debate about STOLI continues. Purists believe that life insurance is meant only for widows, widowers, and orphans. Others say that in a free (STOLI) market—a person can do whatever he or she wishes with his or her policy. Although laws are dealing with this, my view is that the buyer (or seller) should be aware. Don't overinsure. Before ever selling your policies, have an advisor network monitor the transaction step-by-step.

PERMANENT LIFE INSURANCE OPTIONS

The three main kinds of permanent life insurance are *fixed (or guaranteed) whole life, universal life,* and *variable life.* Each policy has cash values. Let's look at them more closely:

1. **Fixed whole life.** This is so solid, it's considered the "rock" of the insurance policy business. Fixed whole life policies feature a guaranteed premium that can never go up and a set death benefit. In other words, if you apply for a $500,000 whole life policy at age 40, you might pay $5,000 a year in premiums. As long as your premiums are paid up and you are careful with cash withdrawals, your beneficiaries will receive $500,000 at your death.

    If you have a traditional fixed whole life policy, your beneficiaries will receive only the death benefit, no matter how much cash value has built up in your account. If you are willing to pay a slightly higher premium, however, you can see to it that your beneficiaries receive the face amount plus extra amounts of insurance, usually referred to as paid-up additions.

2. **Universal life.** These policies have many moving parts, which allow for much more flexibility. After you pay the initial premium, for instance, you can reduce the death benefits or increase them—provided you can prove that your health has not deteriorated. As long as you maintain minimum payment levels, you will have the freedom to vary the timing and the amount of the premiums you pay. If you're flush, for instance, you can pay more; if times are lean, you can pay the minimum amount.

    With these policies, you may be able to get extra interest credits, but there are no guarantees that the premium won't rise.

3. **Variable life.** This policy is dedicated to the stock market and mutual funds. With this kind of insurance, your cash value and death benefit are tied to a mutual fund's investment account. If the funds do well, the cash value and death benefit

can increase. If not, you may have to put in more money to get the death benefit you want. In some cases, you can gain significant policy guarantees.

These policies are worth considering if you're looking at putting money in mutual funds. Ask your financial advisor to run the numbers and show you what you might expect if you buy a variable life policy with a face amount as low as allowable under the law. Since the cash builds tax deferred and can be obtained without taxes, you might have a happier result than if you bought mutual funds directly.

A word of caution: Permanent cash value life insurance can be the ideal place to park serious money over the long term. The system gives so many built-in advantages. However, these policies are not good short-term savings vehicles. The insurance company must recover its costs, and these will come out of your pocket when you cash in early. Become familiar with an insurance agent who can give you straight answers on how these policies can be managed. There is nothing to fear.

WHAT TO CONSIDER WHEN TAPPING INTO CASH VALUES

Let's say you need some quick cash to start up a business or pay emergency medical bills, or for a host of other reasons. Know that you don't need to be approved for an insurance policy loan or fill out a financial statement, either. In most cases, your insurer will get you the money quickly—even overnight, if necessary. Here are basic considerations to keep in mind if you choose to withdraw from—or take a loan against—the cash value in your policy:

1. You can always withdraw or borrow against your cash value. However, any time you take money from your policy, you affect its cash values and death benefits. Your insurance agent

can obtain, in advance, a computer illustration that shows what will happen. If you are good with numbers, the printout itself will be helpful. If not, ask for a step-by-step explanation.

2. If you withdraw less money than you have paid into the policy, you will not be taxed on the withdrawal.

3. If your cash value exceeds what you have paid in premiums and you choose to withdraw an amount that is higher than what you paid in premiums, you will have to pay taxes on the difference. For instance, if you've paid $25,000 in premiums and have accumulated $30,000 in cash values and you choose to withdraw $26,000, you will pay taxes on $1,000 ($26,000 minus the $25,000 you paid in premiums). Notice, however, that in this instance, you will have $4,000 of profit that is still untaxed. It will stay that way until you withdraw it or the contract is cancelled.

4. Withdrawing money could reduce your death benefit dollar for dollar. It all depends on the contract terms in your policy and the level of cash value. For instance, if your death benefit is $500,000 and you withdraw $10,000 from your $25,000 cash value, your death benefit would normally be reduced to $490,000.

5. In some policies, the death benefit could be reduced by more than the amount you withdraw. Again, it depends on the contract.

6. You can take loans against the policy (basically to its total cash value). There is no obligation to pay the money back. However, if you don't, the insurance company will deduct the amount of the loan plus interest from the death benefit. Yes, there is interest on policy loans. Why would the

insurance company charge you interest on borrowing your "own" money? Because the company calculated the annual premium under the assumption that the account would earn interest. Without that interest, premiums would be much higher. Therefore, if you borrow, any lost earnings must be replaced. The good news, however, is that the insurance company will return some of those earnings as interest is credited. Or it could make things simpler and charge zero percent interest and credit zero in return. A contract illustration will give you the information.

7. If you have accumulated enough cash value, you can use the cash in the contract to automatically cover your premium payments.

8. In some cases, your policy will be a "single premium" contract. (For instance, instead of paying 20 annual premiums of $10,000 for a $500,000 policy, you agree to put in, say, a one-time $130,000 single premium. Essentially, $130,000 becomes the present value (PV) of the death benefit—a future value (FV). (Refer again to chapter 1 for a complete explanation of PVs and FVs.) Your goal might be to obtain very little coverage with the lowest possible assessment for mortality costs. Review the policy's contract illustration carefully and look for the term *Modified Endowment Contract* (MEC). If your policy meets the definition of a MEC, all distributions will be taxed LIFO—"interest first" instead of premiums first. Take the situation (in number 3), where a distribution of $26,000 causes taxes to be paid on $1,000. If this policy is an MEC, the $26,000 payment will cause taxes on $5,000 because at the time of the MEC distribution, there was $5,000 of profit in the policy.

9. If your policy is an MEC, loans are treated as distributions and are also taxed interest first. In the situation in number 8, assume that the $26,000 payment is a policy loan from an MEC. Although policy loans are normally tax free, here you'll pay taxes on $5,000 of profit as if this is a withdrawal.

This explains the basics of cash value life insurance policies. In the next chapter on life insurance, I will show you specific strategies that use life insurance policies—on yourself or those in whom you have an "insurable interest"—to boost income in retirement.

LIFE INSURANCE: ADVANCED PLANNING STRATEGIES FOR MORE INCOME IN RETIREMENT

Money is something you have to make
in case you don't die.
—*Max Asnas*

Now that you understand the basics of permanent cash value life insurance, let's look at how to use it to increase retirement income for yourself or a loved one.

STRATEGY 1: A POLICY INSURING A RELATIVE'S LIFE

This can be an excellent way to grow retirement income in a tax-advantaged, asset-protected account at a low cost. Better yet, it's simple. Think about the people in your life in whom you might have—from the insurance company's point of view—a legitimate insurable interest. Is there someone who is younger, healthier, and likely to get better rates than you *and* agreeable to having you take out a policy on his or her life? A younger spouse or sibling maybe?

A child who will take over the policy for his or her family some-day? Or even a parent or in-law, whose untimely death would cause financial loss to your family?

If so, consider purchasing cash value life insurance on that person. As the policyowner, you will be able to use the accumulated cash values to draw an income in retirement. Work closely with your insurance agent to find the right policy. It really doesn't so much matter what kind—whole life, universal life, or variable life. What counts more is the insurance carrier's quality and reputation for treating policyholders fairly, the competitive history of its policies, and the knowledge and helpfulness of its staff. I'd also look at the insurer's guarantees and rankings from A.M. Best, Moody's, and the other ratings agencies I mentioned in the last chapter. You can get this information from your agent or online.

Taking out insurance on a parent could be a great choice. It worked out very well for Joseph, age 45. Joe asked if he should buy insurance on his 65-year-old father to generate the cash he'd need for taxes when his father died—taxes on his father's estate, IRA, and annuities.

I liked the idea. "Since you'll own the policy, the proceeds should be free of any estate taxes and income taxes," I said. "If you don't need the money for your father's taxes, this could be an excellent way to safely increase your retirement income. If you decide you would like to draw an income *and* cover those taxes, you'll need a policy with a higher face amount."

Joe said that he and his wife contribute $5,000 each—for a total of $10,000—to IRA programs. They have an additional $10,000 they can use for an annual premium. I recommended that they purchase a $500,000 permanent policy insuring Joe's father. If, for example, he dies when he is age 85 and Joe is age 65, Joe will receive

$500,000 in tax free insurance proceeds. And Joe will then have about a 20-year life expectancy.

Instead of taking a lump sum, Joe could annuitize/amortize this—at 5 percent or so, into $40,000 a year in retirement income. How long will the payments last? That depends on whether he chooses a life only, term certain, or life annuity with a term certain. Those are payout possibilities I will explain in the next two chapters on annuities.

The tax burden would be relatively light. Consider that the total payout is $800,000 (20 annual payments of $40,000) and the tax-free face amount is $500,000. (The payout over 20 years exceeds the face amount by $300,000, because of interest, at, say, 5 percent, that is credited on the unpaid balance.) To determine how much of the payout is tax free, divide the face amount ($500,000) by the total anticipated payout ($800,000). Since $500,000 ÷ $800,000 is 62.5 percent, then 62.5 percent of each payment is tax free. In short, Joe won't be taxed LIFO. He'll pay taxes on 37.5 percent of each $40,000 payment. In a 30 percent tax bracket, his annual taxes would be $4,500 on taxable income of $15,000.

If Joe arranges this settlement option plan (which I will explain in detail in chapter 10), there's a good chance that payments will be protected from his father's creditors and his own. In brief, this plan pays income over time, instead of in one lump sum payment.

Not bad, eh? For 20 years of paying $10,000 in annual insurance premiums (a present value), Joe would eventually receive over $35,500 annually ($40,000–$4,500) after taxes for, say, 20 years (a future value). It will probably be safeguarded from lawsuits or other claims against it too. How good a return is that? Well, think back to chapter 1 and see if you can guess the approximate annual internal rate of return—or the geometric rate of return—after taxes. (I'll give you the answer a little later on.)

STRATEGY 2: CONVERTING A USELESS POLICY INTO SOMETHING YOU CAN USE

Perhaps you already have a life insurance policy—but you no longer need it. Should you cash it in, or is there a better way to profit from it?

Ann asked this question. She owned a $1 million cash value life insurance policy on a business partner who was no longer with the family business. Ann believed that the policy had served its purpose. She wondered what her options were.

I told her she had several. In brief, she could surrender the policy, donate it to charity and take a tax deduction, exchange it for an annuity, or sell it to a third-party for fair market value—provided that her former partner consents and is willing to sign any life settlement papers.

Let's look more closely at these options.

Let's say Ann paid $100,000 in premiums on a $1 million permanent insurance policy that has accumulated $150,000 in cash value.

On surrender, Ann would have to pay taxes on a profit of $50,000 (the $150,000 in cash value minus $100,000 paid in premiums). To avoid paying taxes, she could assign the policy *tax free* to the same company or another insurance carrier for a $150,000 single premium deferred annuity (SPDA). That would allow money to accumulate tax deferred in the SPDA policy. (For more on SPDAs, see chapters 6 and 7.) Only withdrawals above $100,000—Ann's "tax basis" in the policy—would be taxable.

(Now, suppose cash values were only $80,000. That's a loss, since Ann paid $100,000 in premiums. Unfortunately, that loss is not tax deductible. But if Ann and her father were to transfer the $80,000 policy into an SPDA, future accumulation—from $80,000 up to $100,000—would be tax free!)

Alternately, Ann could assign the policy (worth $150,000) *tax free* in exchange for a $150,000 single premium immediate annuity (SPIA) that credits, say, 5 percent interest as it is annuitized. The annuity pays $12,000 a year for the next 20 years, for a total payout of $240,000. Again, her tax basis is $100,000. Here, $5,000 or 41.67 percent of each payment would be tax free ($100,000 ÷ $240,000). Another option: Ann could donate the policy to charity. She would owe taxes on a profit of $50,000, but the policy's full $150,000 could be a tax deduction. Then, if her tax rate is 30 percent, she'll save $45,000 in income taxes on some other income.

ANSWER TO THE PROBLEM

If you save $10,000 annually at the beginning of the year for 20 years and then receive $35,500 annually at the end of the year for the next 20 years—all tax free—your annual geometric internal rate of return over 40 years would be right at 6½ percent. Not bad as a long-term retirement income plan!

STRATEGY 3: MAKING THE MOST OF A POLICY THAT INSURES YOUR OWN LIFE

You can eventually boost your retirement income by acquiring a cash value life insurance policy on your own life. For instance, Mike, age 45, makes a $5,000 maximum contribution to a Roth IRA. Since he has another $5,000 to spare each year, he could put it toward cash value life insurance. This is another $5,000 "no deduction with interest earnings tax free" program. You could call his policy a "Roth Supplement."

Since Mike's goal is cash accumulation, the policy needs to minimize mortality costs that are assessed by the insurer and slow the rate of accumulation. Let's say his policy has the *lowest* face amount allowed by the IRS. In Mike's case, given his age and the premium he is choosing to pay, the minimum face amount should be about $225,000. (If Mike selected a face value less than $225,000, the policy might still provide death benefits that would not be taxable, but distributions of cash value profit would definitely be taxable.)

Assume that Mike's policy would earn about 5 percent interest (before mortality costs and expenses are subtracted from accumulation values). Based on the contract illustration, Mike's policy would build up a cash value of $150,000 if he continued paying a $5,000 premium annually for 20 years. That sum would be available to him at age 65, the year he's likely to retire.

When that year arrives, Mike could surrender the policy for its $150,000 cash value. If so, he'd have to pay income taxes on a $50,000 gain over premiums of $100,000. But that may not be his best option. Mike might make choices based on his current financial circumstances. Depending on what they are, any of the following options might be better for him. For instance, he could:

1. **Continue the premium.** This could be the right choice if he has the cash available and doesn't need the premium money. In another 20 years, at 5 percent interest, the policy's cash values should be about $500,000, after 5 percent interest is credited and mortality costs and expenses are subtracted.

2. **Cancel the premium, but keep the policy intact.** This might be the best choice if he doesn't have the cash available but can afford to wait to draw on the account. In 20 years, the current cash values of $150,000 should increase to about $300,000 after 5 percent interest is credited and mortality costs and expenses are subtracted.

3. **Inquire about Accelerated Death Benefits (ADBs).** This might be necessary if Mike is facing a terminal illness. If this feature is in the policy, the insurer will accelerate death benefits after learning that the insured has been diagnosed with a terminal illness. (As the policy holder and the insured, Mike would keep the contract and prepare to file a claim.)

   Let me give you a real-life example. My friend, a financial planner in Florida, told me she had a client who owned a small $25,000 life policy where the premium was increasing. Meanwhile, he was dying in a nursing home. She discovered a 50 percent ADB in his policy that could pay $12,500 of the insurance *now!* The insurer agreed and gave this to the client. The client used it to pay for the nursing home. The insurer said it would pay the balance on death. Voila! You should have seen her client's face. The $12,500 ADB might seem to be a modest amount, but this little known benefit was a godsend under those circumstances.

4. **Take a maximum policy loan.** This could be an excellent choice if Mike finds a good business or investment opportunity. In that case, he'd borrow cash from the policy or pledge it for a loan at the bank.

5. **Exchange the policy for another life policy.** This might be the best choice if actuarial factors change in 20 years—and I expect that they will. In general, life expectancies will be longer and premiums less. If so, Mike might trade this policy for one with a greater face amount if that would provide more for his family. Under 2009 law, there will be no tax effect with this exchange.

6. **Sell the policy.** Twenty years from now, Mike could be uninsurable or unhealthy. In a life settlement, he might sell the policy and get, say, $200,000 cash or more—something

higher than his cash value of $150,000. Even if he is healthy, the sale could be profitable. He'd need to investigate this carefully before proceeding.

7. **Make an "internal exchange" for an annuity with XYZ, the present carrier.** Say Mike doesn't need the policy, is in a low tax bracket, and wants retirement income. Company XYZ credits 5 percent interest and pays an $11,500 annuity for 20 years, for a total payout of $230,000. Of that total, $130,000 ($230,000 less $100,000 in premiums) is taxable. But the taxes won't amount to that much because of Mike's low tax bracket.

8. **Make an "external exchange" for an annuity with another carrier.** It's possible that Mike could get an even better deal with another company. Let's say Company XYZ pays $11,500 but ABC Co. pays $12,000. If so, Mike can trade in the policy tax free for ABC's higher income.

9. **Take tax free distributions from his original policy.** The contract illustration from Company XYZ shows that when Mike reaches age 66, a $150,000 cash value will pay nearly $10,000 tax free for 20 years from policy loans and withdrawals. If tax brackets then are, say, 50 percent, that equals a $20,000 taxable income. Here, he'd likely take tax free distributions directly from the life policy.

The bottom line: Company XYZ's life contract illustration shows that a $5,000 premium, paid annually over 20 years, builds to nearly $150,000 in cash value. (It also has a $225,000 death benefit.) A Roth IRA at 5 percent interest accumulates more money—$174,000 tax free—but provides nothing extra at death. In this way, the Roth and cash life insurance policy complement each other.

STRATEGY 4: HOW TO HANDLE AN "UNDERPERFORMING" POLICY

Mike's spare cash put him in a fortunate situation. Sometimes, older policyholders have the opposite problem, which can make it difficult for them to hold on to their policies. Recently, Mary asked about her Aunt Mildred, who had purchased a $10,000 annual premium, $1 million life policy some 25 years ago. Mildred's health had deteriorated. The insurance company told the family there wasn't much cash value, and that it would need annual premiums of up to $30,000 to maintain the policy. She wasn't alone. This dilemma has been called the "'Inevitable Policy Crash." I explained that in the 1970s and 80s, interest rates were higher and policy illustrations projected high rates over the long term. Unfortunately, those forecasters were mistaken. Now, many policies are undervalued and in danger of lapsing.

The family needed to obtain a personal actuarial study to learn the current value of Aunt Mildred's policy in the family's estate. Generally, these reports are well worth the money. The actuary would do a thorough study of Aunt Mildred's health and lifestyle and would be able to forecast how many years Aunt Mildred would need a nursing home or assisted living and determine her *individual* life expectancy.

"Why don't you wait on your decision to cancel the policy or pay further premiums until after you have the study done?" I told her. "It may appear that the $1 million policy is worth merely its cash value, which is essentially zero. However, its actual value could be much more for the family." The actuarial study would resolve the matter.

The family had the study done. It placed Mildred's individual life expectancy at 78 years, which is down from the policy's estimate of 85 years. (Apparently, Mildred's health had *really* deteriorated.)

That's a significant difference. The $30,000 annual premium is based on the insurer's assumption that Mildred would have a normal life span of about 85 years. But if her current life expectancy is age 78, these figures were high. Perhaps she should pay in less. If Aunt Mildred decided to continue the contract, the family should work with the insurer to "fine-tune" the numbers.

Actually, if Aunt Mildred wanted to keep the policy, and she had CDs or treasuries, she could "liquidate" them and pay cash into the contract. That way, the money would earn tax free interest. Then she could take tax free withdrawals or policy loans; in effect, she would convert taxable interest into tax free distributions of income in retirement.

Here is how that would look: Let's assume Mildred's $1 million life contract has zero cash value and her $300,000 in CD/treasuries earns 5 percent (or $15,000 annually) in taxable interest. She cashes in the CD/treasuries and deposits $300,000 into the policy. That money now earns tax free interest inside the contract. Then, she takes tax free loans/withdrawals annually for more retirement income.

The bottom line: Aunt Mildred exchanges her CD (and its taxable income) for tax free payments from the policy. Her former CD replenishes her policy's reserve and keeps it from lapsing.

If you have an underperforming policy, you might consider doing the same.

REVERSIONARY ANNUITIES—A SPECIAL KIND OF LIFE INSURANCE

At a later meeting, Mary poses a different question: "My dad Harry is in good health, and he's younger than Aunt Mildred. Although it appears likely that she will die before he does, my dad would like to make sure that she has an income if he dies. What's the best way to arrange this?"

Harry should consider a *reversionary annuity*—an insurance policy where the death benefit is not paid out as a lump sum, but as *lifetime* monthly income to its beneficiary. Premiums are based on the health of both the insured and beneficiary. This kind of insurance has no cash value. But here's the good news: since Mildred has a reduced life expectancy and is older than Harry, this policy won't cost that much. A contract illustration will give the answers. If Mildred predeceases Harry, no income is paid out. Then if he had paid in a slightly higher premium, he would receive back the money he paid in.

Reversionary annuities can work well in these situations. They can cost less than term life insurance. Of course, if Harry was older or more likely to predecease the aunt, he could purchase a conventional life insurance policy.

—

As these examples show, life insurance is a valuable property. Learn to look at it not as a burden, but an *opportunity*. Get familiar with the math, thoroughly explore your options with your financial advisor, and take the time to familiarize yourself with contract illustrations and *all* their possibilities. As I have shown, a policy can do much more than provide death benefits. What counts is how you manage the contract.

Consider, too, that you might be able to get the best return on the dollars you spend on life insurance by insuring someone else. Such policies may be less expensive, and therefore a better value. If you can afford to do so, insure your parents or yourself to build a retirement income fund. And if you have an underperforming policy, don't cash it in before you explore your alternatives. Otherwise, as I showed you in the example, you might lose an excellent opportunity to keep more money in your hands, instead of lapsing the contract in haste.

Finally, consider a low-cost reversionary annuity to guarantee a lifetime "retirement" income for your beneficiary. Not many insurers offer these policies, but they are available as of the date I wrote this chapter.

LIFE INSURANCE: A BRIEF ASSET PROTECTION PLANNING ANALYSIS

Picture this: You own a hefty amount of life insurance cash values. You didn't pay premiums with the intent to fool anyone. Then it happens—a lawsuit comes out of left field. (Your dog bites the neighbor and she wins.) If you are lucky enough to live in one of 10 states that afford full protection to insurance policies, chances are excellent that your neighbor won't be able to get anywhere near your cash values. Surely that should make a stodgy life policy seem better!

While those 10 states offer full protection to all life insurance policies—with a few exceptions—all but two offer at least partial protection. (See "A State-by-State Look at How the Law Safeguards Life Insurance Cash Values as Well as Annuity Cash Values and Death Proceeds" in Appendix A on page 229.)

Many such laws have been in effect for at least a century. And even the U.S. Supreme Court has had its say here, opining in Burnet v. Wells (289 U.S. 760) that life insurance is a pressing social duty to be abandoned only under "dire compulsion." Why does the government care about life insurance? It's very simple. As I mention in chapter 3, if parents don't make some provision for each other or their offspring in the event of an untimely death, that financial burden falls back on society. And that's why all but two U.S. states (and one territory) have enacted legislation meant to significantly safeguard the "proceeds and avails" of life insurance. These are generally recognized as the cash and loan values, policy dividends, and death benefits.

Realize, however, that even in states that offer full protection, the IRS can get its hands on your policy if you owe the IRS money. And in most states, protection isn't extended to those behind on marital obligations such as alimony or child support payments. Asset protection laws can't help you there.

That's clear cut. But there are many instances where it is not immediately obvious who's protected and under what circumstances. If you take out cash values as a loan and pay the loan back, for instance, is the money you returned to the policy account still protected? There are many such questions. That's why you, the policyowner or beneficiary, should ask your insurance agent or lawyer the tough questions up front. *Never* assume something is protected. Find out, and plan accordingly.

These are some excellent questions to ask:

1. "Which state law applies?"
2. "As a policyowner, are my cash values protected from personal creditors?"
3. "As a *beneficiary* of a life insurance policy, how am I protected from creditors of the former (now deceased) insured, the policyowner (if other than the insured), my creditors, or all of our creditors?"
4. "What happens when death proceeds (or cash values) leave the insurer and get to someone's checking account? Are these funds sheltered then and thereafter?"
5. "If I want to negotiate/arrange a settlement action plan for a beneficiary, should I do this before I die?"
6. "If I get into financial trouble, can someone say I paid premiums to defraud creditors?"

You need up-to-date answers, specific to the state in which you live. That's why I suggest you pose these questions to your insurance agent or attorney. In Appendix A on page 229, I will provide some general answers for you, according to my analysis of *current law*. Realize, however, that there could have been significant changes in the law since this book went to press.

In summary then, a life policy's specific creditor-protection laws are significant. You never know when a claim, lawsuit, or even bankruptcy will surface. If cash values and death proceeds are safeguarded, it can make a whopping difference. Check out settlement options and see how insurance proceeds and avails can be sheltered in your state. Every time you pay a life premium, think affirmatively; you could be assembling value that's difficult for others to reach.

ANNUITIES: THE BASICS

The time to save is now. When a dog gets a bone,
he doesn't go out and make a down payment on a
bigger bone. He buries the one he's got.
—*Will Rogers*

Annuities—at their most basic—are contracts you purchase from an insurer in exchange for income. *Webster's New World Dictionary* defines an annuity as "a payment of a fixed sum of money at regular intervals of time, especially years." Your insurance agent might also define an annuity as an insurance contract that allows savings to accumulate efficiently in a tax-deferred account. Both are correct, even if the definitions are a bit simplistic.

There are different kinds of annuity contracts, each suited to a specific purpose or goal. Some are designed to build wealth for retirement; others to systematically liquidate the buildup and create guaranteed income for life. The payout annuity (which I will discuss mostly in the next chapter) is an example of the latter. It is the only financial instrument—besides Social Security—that guarantees an income you can't outlive. If you've ever wondered how to make sure you don't run out of money before you die—even if you live many years beyond actuarial projections—annuities are your answer.

I adore annuities because they offer income safeguards and guarantees, tax deferral, asset protection, and other valuable features. There isn't anything else that offers this package of features. I can't imagine building a comprehensive retirement income plan without them. Nor should you. Annuities, like cash value life insurance, need to be a cornerstone of any such plan.

In this chapter and the next, I'll show you why. We'll start by looking at one simple way you can come out ahead with annuities. Then, I'll explain the advantages and drawbacks of various types of annuities and introduce you to progressively more advanced planning techniques.

—

Within the world of annuities there are fixed annuities, which offer a guaranteed rate of return, and variable annuities, which introduce risk and may bring potentially higher returns. One place fixed annuities shine, for instance, is as an alternative to other so-called safe investments such as certificates of deposit (CDs), treasuries, and bonds. Here's an example. Marvin and Pearl have $100,000 they can afford to set aside for 20 years. They're both age 55, so they don't want the money at risk, but they do want the best return they can get. What should they do?

I quickly review the facts. Marvin and Pearl are in a 30 percent tax bracket, so an instrument that maximizes tax savings is ideal. I know they are intelligent savers. Since they have enough set aside elsewhere for unexpected emergencies, they can afford to let this money sit untouched. Given those facts, and their desire for low risk, I suggest a $100,000 fixed annuity (a *single premium deferred annuity* or *SPDA*) crediting 5 percent interest per annum. Let's say

Marvin owns the policy. The contract will mature in 40 years—at his 95th birthday—but cash withdrawals can begin earlier. (I am using 5 percent interest for 40 years to age 95 to make this example easier to understand mathematically; typically, annuity policies mature when an individual turns age 85 or 90.) The only catch: Marvin will have to leave the $100,000 in the annuity for at least 10 years, or face "surrender charges"—a penalty on withdrawals or an early cash in.

Marvin and Pearl intend to keep the money in the annuity for 20 years. If they do (and if the contract continues to credit 5 percent interest), the account will grow to about $265,300, which represents a $165,300 profit on their original "investment." If they choose to cash in the entire annuity that year, and they're still in a 30 percent tax bracket, they'll have to pay taxes of about $50,000 (30 percent) on the $165,300 profit. That will leave Marvin and Pearl with $215,000, which is $15,000 more than they would earn if they had put the $100,000 into a 5 percent CD, treasury, or bond instead.

What accounts for that difference?

The other savings vehicles provide the same 5 percent interest, but the interest in each case is subject to annual taxes. When a 30 percent tax is deducted from the earnings, the actual annual rate drops to merely 3.5 percent net. That slows the growth. With the annuity, however, the tax is deferred during the accumulation years. Because that money stays in the account—instead of going to the IRS—the interest is calculated based on a larger sum. The money is treated as if it belongs to the policyowner, not the IRS.

There are other tax advantages as well. Marvin and Pearl don't have to wait 20 years to access their money; nor are they required to take any withdrawals before the contract reaches its maturity date another 20 years out. (With annuities, there are no requirements to start taking minimum distributions at age 70½, as there are with Individual Retirement Accounts.) This gives them a great deal of leeway, so they can take advantage of any changes in tax circumstances.

If, for instance, Marvin's income drops and his deductions increase dramatically, he can withdraw money from the annuity, time everything perfectly, and conceivably avoid all income taxes. Or he can make a tax free exchange for a new contract that pays out income or convert the existing contract to payout mode, spreading out the income payments—and tax obligations—over a number of years, or his full life expectancy. He might even choose a payout for as long as either he or Pearl live.

Alternately, the couple can keep money in the annuity until the maturity date, deferring taxes for up to 40 years and building even more wealth at a faster rate than other "safe" investments. If they opt for this, the sum will increase to about $705,000 at the contract's maturity date. Then, they'll have to pay taxes of about $180,000 on a $605,000 profit, leaving them with $525,000. This is $125,000 more than they'd earn if the money was placed directly in CDs, treasuries, or bonds.

The tax deferral could continue even longer for Marvin's and Pearl's beneficiaries. Let's say that Marvin dies before the contract reaches its maturity date. At that point, the annuity contract passes to Pearl, his beneficiary. She can elect to leave the money in the account and continue the tax deferral. If she also dies before the contract reaches its maturity date (the date at which Marvin would have reached age 95), her beneficiaries would normally have 60 days after her death to cash out and pay taxes, or they could annuitize—take the payments over time—and pay taxes gradually over their lifetimes. At age 65, they could spread the tax payments out for 20 more years.

That's 50 or 60 years of tax-deferred income growth! From a pure tax planning perspective, what could be better?

—

That's just a single, simple example of the tax savings power of annuities. As you may have surmised, there are two broad categories of annuity contracts: accumulation (which account for over 95 percent of the annuity marketplace) and payout. Marvin and Pearl bought an accumulation annuity—more specifically, a *fixed-rate* accumulation annuity—as a safe way to build tax-deferred wealth for retirement.

Let's take a closer look at the features, strengths, and drawbacks of fixed accumulation annuities. In the next chapter, I'll discuss payout policies in more detail.

FIXED ACCUMULATION ANNUITIES

A fixed accumulation annuity works a bit like a savings account. There typically is no front-end sales charge. All the money earns a set rate of interest and builds in value over time. However, you give your deposit(s) to the insurance company, not the bank. Instead of getting a savings passbook, you get a contract, which spells out your obligations to the insurer and its obligations to you.

For instance, you basically agree to leave the money in the annuity for a set period of time. This allows the insurer to make long-term investments in bonds and other fixed-income securities, earning interest income at favorable rates, most of which end up in your account. The contract will specify the minimum amount of time you must keep money in the annuity if you don't want to pay a "surrender charge" for withdrawals. The contract will also name a maturity date, at which point your deposit and all interest credited to your contract over the years will return to you.

With this kind of annuity, the insurer guarantees a fixed interest rate for a specified period, and also promises that (a) the annuity's principal is guaranteed, (b) interest when credited becomes principal, and (c) certain other rates and costs will be maintained. In other words, there will be no surprises.

If you buy an accumulation annuity with a single payment, it is called a *single premium deferred annuity (SPDA)*. Alternately, you can make periodic deposits at regular intervals, in which case it is called a *flexible premium deferred annuity*. Either can become a payout annuity later on.

Why Annuities Are a Safe Place to Stash Cash

All fixed annuities are fully guaranteed by insurance carriers, but there is no Federal Deposit Insurance Corporation (FDIC) insurance or backing by the U.S. government. However, states do regulate and oversee insurance companies, the products they market, and the practices they follow. Each state has an insurance commissioner who monitors and licenses agents and listens to consumer complaints. In addition, insurers in each state contribute to insurance guaranty associations that protect residents.

These associations assure personal annuity guaranteed values—$100,000 to $500,000 per individual life—if a carrier fails. (As of December 31, 2008, for instance, there were 40 state guaranty associations that protected up to $100,000 in a resident's annuity cash surrender values; another 10 states provided protection ranging from $200,000 to $500,000.) Because payout annuities don't have cash surrender values, they usually have higher coverage limits than accumulation annuities. This coverage limit will typically apply to the "present value of guaranteed future annuity payments." You'll have to check to see if that's true in your state.

If an insurer can't pay its debts, these associations assess healthy carriers to build a payment fund. State insurance departments will work out a plan with guaranty associations that could involve rehabilitation. If a company finally fails, another carrier could assume control and protect a policyholder's contract and its values. If that can't be worked out, the company is liquidated and each state's Guaranty Fund provides a security blanket for its residents.

All carriers doing business in your state (and the troubled carrier's state) must back the troubled carrier's insurance and annuity policies and its commitments. Even if the investment bank the insurance company invests in goes broke, your policy will make good on its guarantees.

Given all of these layers of protection, I consider fixed annuities "boxes full of safe money." They are worth considering when you are looking for the safety you'd expect from a certificate of deposit, treasury, or bond. To help you choose a sound and profitable insurance company, personally review how independent agencies such as A.M. Best, Standard & Poor's, Moody's, Fitch, and Weiss rate the carriers. Google these agencies and the insurance carriers and ask your insurance agent for up-to-date reports.

WHAT YOU CAN DO IF YOUR INSURER FAILS

Yes, insurers can fail. If this happens to you, contact your state insurance department—then relax. They'll tell you what's happening and what to do; you won't lack information. Insurance agents (and representatives of the insurance carrier) will also advise and help.

What's the worst that can happen? What if another insurance company doesn't assume the deal you bargained for when you bought your annuity contract? You might cash out up to the sum guaranteed by the insurance guaranty association in your state. You could keep your contract and receive at least the minimum rate of interest guaranteed in the contract. Know that you will likely come out with an above-average arrangement after the restructuring.

What are the chances of losing money in a fixed annuity arrangement? There's little cause for concern here. As noted annuity author Jack Marrion said to financial planners in his June 2009 column for *Senior Market Advisor* magazine: "You can't tell consumers that no one has ever lost money in a fixed annuity due to carrier failure, because they have, but you can tell them this: From 1994 through 2008, there were 94 bank failures. During the same period, customers of a little over a dozen interstate annuity carriers received cash from state guaranty funds. Every state guaranty fund covered at least $100,000 of cash value, and there were only three failed carriers that did not provide all of the account value for all of their customers—an even better record for the period than FDIC."

Comparing Fixed Annuities to Conventional Savings Plans

Savers who want safe and secure returns typically choose CDs; treasury instruments (bonds, notes, and certificates) or treasuries; top-rated bond mutual funds; or some combination of these. As I showed you at the start of this chapter, Marvin and Pearl could also use fixed accumulation annuities to amass some serious cash in a tax-deferred account. For the purpose of comparing fixed accumulation annuities to these better-known savings vehicles—in greater detail than before—let's imagine you have $200,000 to set aside and you are in a 30 percent tax bracket.

For convenience, let's also assume that these conventional savings vehicles provide typical interest earnings of 5 percent.

Certificates of deposit (CDs)

CDs (and money market deposits) are attractive because these are backed (or insured) up to $250,000 per account by the FDIC, at least until December 31, 2013, when this amount is scheduled to revert to $100,000. (The FDIC does *not* insure safety deposit boxes, mutual funds, annuities, stocks, bonds, treasuries, securities, and other investments.) To insure any more money in a CD, you must go to another bank for the excess. Be aware that CDs have charges for early surrenders. However, the cost is fairly low. For instance, the charge might be 6 months of earned interest. (If a 5 percent CD worth $100,000 was surrendered early, that charge could be about $2,500.) Some have call features where the issuing bank can terminate the CD and return your money before the maturity date. The other downside: CDs have neither income tax advantages nor personal creditor protection under state laws. Assuming a 30 percent tax rate over 1 year, you will earn $10,000 pre-tax and $7,000 after-tax returns from a 5 percent, $200,000 CD.

U.S. treasuries

Treasury instruments are loans to the federal government for its projects. They are backed by the "full faith and credit" of the U.S. government and are extremely low risk. They are not callable and carry the advertised interest rate to maturity. If interest rates rise, the instrument's present resale value will fall. Interest earned is included on your tax return; however, it is only subject to federal taxes. Except for the state income tax break, treasuries have neither income tax advantages nor personal creditor protection under state laws. Assuming a 30 percent tax rate, you will earn $10,000 pre-tax and $7,000 after-tax returns from $200,000 invested in 5 percent treasuries.

A bond mutual fund

A managed fund that invests in high-grade corporate bonds will fluctuate due to changes in interest rates and rating agency downgrades/upgrades of the bonds. Also, there is no investor FDIC insurance protection. A small portion of the total bond fund income might be taxed at favorable capital gains rates. However, there are no tax advantages, nor is there personal creditor protection. Assuming a 30 percent tax rate, you will have $10,000 pretax and basically a $7,000 after-tax income from $200,000 in bond mutual fund shares that earn 5 percent. Unlike treasuries and some CDs, most bond funds will permit investors to accumulate interest by automatically reinvesting it into the fund.

Here are the 20-year economics of these three $200,000 conventional savings possibilities: In each situation, I'll assume that you will earn $10,000 annually and $7,000 net after paying a $3,000 income tax. In 20 years, you will have $200,000, plus what you have kept of $140,000 in net interest earnings. If you reinvested that interest, you will accrue what is earned on this as well.

Assume that you reinvest $7,000 each year for 20 years at 3½ percent interest (after paying taxes at 30 percent on 5 percent in interest earnings). You would accrue roughly $200,000 in overall interest earnings, bringing your total to $400,000.

Now let's compare that to the 20-year economics of a $200,000 single premium deferred annuity also earning 5 percent. After 20 years, the contract will be worth $530,000. Of course, you will still owe taxes on $330,000 ($530,000 less $200,000) of accumulated interest in the annuity. If you're still in a 30 percent bracket and you have to pay taxes on the whole sum, you'll owe $99,000, leaving you with $431,000. (If you're in a lower tax bracket, then obviously you will get to keep more of your money.)

Accumulation Annuities Compared to Conventional Savings Vehicles for a $200,000 Initial Investment (Rounded to the Nearest $1,000)

	Annual Taxes on Profit?	Annual Return	Taxes Paid at 30%	Gross After 20 Years	Net After 20 Years
5% CD and earnings reinvested at 5% interest	Yes	3.5 % net, after taxes of 30 % are paid on profit	$3,000 annually, or $60,000 over 20 years, plus taxes on reinvested earnings	$400,000—taxes are already paid	a $200,000 CD, plus net of $200,000 earnings over 20 years
5% Treasury	Yes	Same	Same	Same	Same
5% Bond	Yes	Same	Same	Same	Same
5% Fixed accumulation annuity	No—only on payout	5%—no taxes are paid while money remains in account	$99,000 if cashed in after 20 years	$530,000—taxes still to be paid	$431,000 if cashed in after 20 years, and taxes are paid

If you compare the conventional savings plans to an annuity contract, with the exception of the bond mutual fund and CDs in my examples, you'll see that conventional savings plans—predominantly treasuries—tend to be cumbersome because their interest credits usually must be redeployed outside in some other savings instruments. Accumulation annuity policies are more convenient ways to accumulate capital since their tax-deferred interest credits are automatically kept indefinitely within the contract. In fact, it's common for financial planners to note that "in an annuity contract, you earn tax-deferred interest, tax-deferred interest on that interest, and tax-deferred interest on the taxes you don't pay over the years." In other words, annuity contracts are safe, worry-free, and income tax efficient.

While CDs and bond mutual funds usually permit the reinvestment of interest credits within an account, you still receive a Form 1099 that currently taxes these earnings. With an accumulation annuity, your insurer won't send a Form 1099 until you withdraw the interest.

Comparing Asset Protection Features of Annuities with Conventional Savings Plans

Choosing a fixed or variable annuity over the more conventional savings vehicles can be advantageous in other ways too. In more than one-third of the states, annuity values are fully safeguarded from creditors and lawsuits. Another third offer some shelter. You generally won't find this protection afforded to real estate, stocks, bonds, and other conventional investments.

There are situations in which such asset protection can come in handy. Consider the Enron debacle, where CEO Kenneth and Mrs. Lay reportedly acquired up to $10 million in variable annuities far ahead of his company's money problems. Under Texas law, annuity cash values are exempt from creditors if premiums aren't paid with intent to defraud, hinder, or delay adversaries. If the Lays could meet that test, they'd have some serious money that no one could attach or garnishee.

Someday, such protection might prove useful for you and/or your beneficiaries. (Yes, asset protection laws can protect beneficiaries too, so make sure your beneficiary designations are up-to-date.) If you, the annuity owner, are sued for any reason—in a state that provides full protection—you cannot lose your annuity funds to the person who is suing you, with a few exceptions. If you owe taxes to the IRS or child support, for instance, your annuity funds could be seized. If you are the beneficiary who is undergoing a divorce proceeding, however, a court will trace the source of this inheritance and may protect it from your spouse.

Drawbacks of Accumulation Annuities

Certainly, accumulation annuities have their advantages over more conventional savings vehicles. But I wouldn't be giving you the full picture unless I explained the drawbacks too. Here are a few to consider:

1. **Accumulation annuities generally don't keep pace with inflation.** With a fixed contract, you'll probably lose to inflation. That's true with CDs, treasuries, and bonds too. It's a matter of looking at things carefully with your skillful advisor. To adjust for inflation, a fixed payout annuity can add a cost-of-living (COL) rider. (Or a variable accumulation or payout contract with its upside potential can provide an inflation hedge.) There is always a cost; ask an agent to give you the details behind a few COL riders.

2. **There may be low fixed renewal interest rates.** Let's say Company XYZ sells a single premium tax-deferred fixed annuity that can be cashed in without a surrender charge after 10 years. The company offers an attractive 5 percent fixed interest rate for the first 5 years of the annuity and specifies that the renewal fixed interest rate for each 5-year period will be at least 2 percent interest. After 5 years, the company could drop your interest rate to, say, the minimum of 2 percent while offering 5 percent interest rates to those who buy new annuities. The company's conduct is not illegal or immoral. However, upon renewal, a good carrier should endeavor to credit more than its minimum rate guarantee. Before purchasing a contract, ask the insurance company for a historical record of its renewal and current rates. Then, make your buying decision.

3. **Commissions for fixed policies seem too high!** Typical commissions for fixed policies are 1 to 8 percent in the 1st year or a series of small "trailer" payments over the years. Generally, I think this compensation is fair and normally isn't charged to your policy as a front-end load. Insurance agents work hard and deal with tough real-life issues. There isn't any prize for time spent when sales are lost; commissions aren't negotiable and are an agents' only direct financial reward. You want a fairly paid agent who will still be around when you need help. You don't want someone who must leave the insurance business.

4. **Expect to pay "surrender charges" if you withdraw or cash in early.** Let's say your $100,000 accumulation annuity has grown to $120,000. There is a 10 percent surrender charge but also a 10 percent penalty free withdrawal privilege each year. You ask for $20,000. You can get $12,000 (10 percent

of $120,000) penalty free. You will have to pay a 10 percent surrender charge of $800 on the remaining $8,000. Ultimately, the insurance company sends you a check for $19,200 ($20,000 less $800).

Surrender charges can be constructive. They discourage withdrawals and cashing in early. Without surrender charges, there would be more front-end loads. And carriers are more likely to optimize earnings on their investments if they can depend on money staying in their policies.

The surrender charges and any penalty-free withdrawals are spelled out in both sales literature and the contract. Insurance agents are required to discuss them, and your contract information will include a home office phone number to call with any questions. There also is a 15 to 30 day "free-look" period to cancel the contract after it is delivered. This depends on your state's law. During this time, you can return the contract with a money-back guarantee. Insurance companies want you to be happy with your purchase.

The bottom line: Read the fine print and ask agents questions about surrender charges. Policyholders are entitled to an accurate explanation of what can happen when there is an assessment. But know that eventually these charges expire. If you need emergency money in the meantime, a good personal line of credit or source of money helps. Unless there is no other alternative, I caution you to leave money in policies during the surrender charge period.

More General Cautions

Earlier in the chapter, I spoke about how the $100,000 tax-deferred annuity I recommended for Marvin and Pearl could keep the tax man at bay for decades, even for their heirs. That's true, but only if their beneficiaries are on the ball about the 60-day rule.

The bottom line: Nonspouse beneficiaries have only 60 days from the date of the annuitant or policyholder's death to convert the accumulation into a payout annuity and extend taxes on any profit. If they don't act within 60 days of that date (as usually specified in the contract), and the lump sum becomes payable, taxes are due on any profits. On the 61st day, it's too late to annuitize and spread taxes over the years ahead.

Another caution: From purely a tax perspective, in most cases, trusts aren't the best beneficiary for an annuity contract for several reasons. The first is that a trust currently pays income taxes at the highest rates. The second is that some insurance carriers won't give income options to trusts. But that is not always the case.

More Fun with Accumulation Annuities

For simplicity's sake, in the previous text, I focused on a specific kind of accumulation annuity: fixed annuities. Part of my purpose was to show how these perform compared to other so-called safe savings vehicles.

Not all accumulation annuities provide a true fixed rate of return, however. Single premium deferred annuities—which we have focused on in this chapter—can also be fixed, indexed, or variable.

As I said earlier, true fixed accumulation annuities provide straightforward, guaranteed rates of return. These annuities have cash surrender values that don't diminish—even when interest rates change. Indexed annuities offer the possibility of enhanced interest. Variable contracts provide variable returns based on mutual funds. They have minimum guarantees; I have noticed that the guarantees seem to be diminishing.

Let's look a little more closely at each.

With *true fixed* annuities, a carrier typically contractually promises competitive interest rates (4 or 5 percent or so annually in 2009 and 2010) for a specific period such as 5 years. Then, it renews the promise at a new fixed rate for another period. (Again, the minimum rate is specified in the contract, so you'll know it beforehand.) Typical surrender charges might be 8-8-8-7-7 percent over a 5-year period.

Fixed indexed annuities are very creative savings vehicles. Here's a situation that illustrates how they work:

Let's say John pays $150,000 for Company XYZ's fixed indexed contract that promises a modest $165,000 cash-out in 10 years. To assure its obligation, XYZ invests $100,000 (from John's $150,000 premium) in 5 percent treasuries that will accumulate in 10 years time to that $165,000. Once these bonds are set aside, XYZ has $50,000 ($150,000 less $100,000) that can acquire options in, say, the Standard & Poor's Index. If the index goes up over the 10 years, John's annuity will be credited with excess interest as spelled out in the contract.

Typically John's contract will have a cap (say 6 to 10 percent annually) on exactly how much of any profit can be credited as interest. Once there is an interest credit, the "gain" is locked in for any future credits. For instance, a $150,000 fixed indexed contract (which can't lose money) credits 6 percent interest and grows to $159,000 in value; then any new interest credits are applied to $159,000, and so on.

If the index goes down, the options will expire and nothing will happen. John knows that 10 years out, he'll still have $165,000, at the very least.

The bottom line: After 10 years, John will have the higher of (a) $165,000 or (b) the accumulation of $150,000 with its interest credits. If those credits were, say, 6 percent each year, then (b) would be $269,000 after 10 years.

Realize, however, that in a fixed indexed contract, the indexes might be "flat" over several years where you receive zero in interest credits. Here, a true fixed contract would have paid, say, its 4, 5, or 6 percent interest (but with no possibility of extra interest credits). In other words, if the market is flat or goes down, you lose on the indexed annuity because you only get 1 or 2 percent interest, not the 5 percent rate of a true fixed annuity, as in my examples.

Variable policies invest your annuity in mutual funds rather than index options. There is market risk, but you can choose guarantees at an extra cost. These include minimum interest credits and guaranteed annual lifetime withdrawal benefits (GLWBs). I'll discuss GLWBs more fully in chapter 7.

Now that you understand some basics about how accumulation annuities can help you build "up the ladder"—as some say—let's move ahead. In the next chapter, I will show you progressively more advanced planning techniques that will allow you to choose payout annuities "down the ladder" for spectacular results. I will also explain the use of another kind of annuity—the single premium deferred immediate annuity (SPDIA)—that combines the features of both.

A GLOSSARY

Annuity: Traditionally, this is a contract you purchase from an insurer in exchange for income. At present, an annuity is more likely to be a contract that accumulates tax-deferred interest.

Annuitize: This means to convert a lump sum, at a fixed price, into a stream of predetermined income, paid over a period of time. Usually, this election is irrevocable.

Accumulation annuity: This is a type of annuity that builds wealth over time in a tax-deferred account.

Fixed annuity: This type of annuity offers a guaranteed rate of return for a specified period of time.

Fixed indexed annuity: This kind of annuity could promise a lower guaranteed interest rate (say 1 or 2 percent) than a true fixed annuity but give the possibility of an enhanced or extra interest rate credit.

Maturity date: This date, specified in the annuity contract, is the date that your deposit and all interest credited in the contract is returned to you, along with your premium payments. But you can always gain access to your money; maturity dates have nothing to do with limits on withdrawals or a cash-out of your policy. Typically, annuity policies mature when an individual turns age 85 or 90.

Payout annuity: This kind of annuity can help you turn a single large sum of money into a steady stream of income. (See *single premium immediate annuity* and *annuitize.*)

Single premium deferred annuity (SPDA): This is an annuity that is purchased with a single payment and used to accumulate cash surrender values over time. Later, it gives payout annuity rates per $1,000 of cash surrender value. (See *annuitize.*) Normally, there are no restrictions on when these policies can be annuitized.

Single premium immediate annuity (SPIA): This is an annuity used to begin a payout income immediately.

Single premium deferred immediate annuity (SPDIA): This kind of annuity has features of both deferred and immediate annuities. It performs like a deferred annuity until the agreed payout date (unless smaller, earlier payments are also part of the contract) and then functions like payout annuities, once converted into an income. Typically, there is no cash surrender value.

Variable annuity: This is a type of annuity that introduces market risk and may bring potentially higher returns than a true fixed-rate annuity. A variable annuity could also produce lower policy values.

ANNUITIES: ADVANCED PLANNING STRATEGIES FOR MORE INCOME IN RETIREMENT

The two most beautiful words in the English language
are "check enclosed."
—*Dorothy Parker*

When most people think about retirement income planning, they tend to focus on *accumulating* assets. That's only half the picture. If you want to build secure, lifelong income, you also have to be smart about *liquidating* assets in retirement. This is where "payout" annuities excel. Although they represent a much smaller share of the market than accumulation annuities, they are absolutely worth your consideration. Many experts, including one of my favorite financial writers, syndicated columnist Humberto Cruz, recommend using payout annuities to generate 30 to 40 percent of your retirement income.

Payout annuities are issued only by insurance companies and are sometimes referred to as "income" annuities, with good reason. They can help you turn a single large sum of money into a steady stream of income. If the annuity is purchased with a single sum and pays an immediate income, it is called a *single premium immediate annuity* or SPIA (pronounced spee-ah). The first payment might come within a month, but if not, it will definitely start within the next 12 months. Like SPDAs (the single premium deferred annuities I spoke of in the previous chapter), SPIAs offer the option of fixed-rate or variable-rate contracts. The first provides the advantage of knowing exactly how much income your annuity will earn and pay out each year. The second may help you keep pace with inflation by investing in the financial markets.

Let's make this concrete by looking at how a payout contract works.

Paul, age 65, tells me he has $200,000 he would like to convert into a series of income payments. His goal? To create more cash flow *now* without sacrificing safety.

He could amortize the $200,000 himself, but that's difficult given the income reinvestment issues and tax ramifications I discussed in chapter 6. Since safety is a concern, one option is a fixed payout annuity that, presumably, credits a *guaranteed* return of, say, 5 percent on the "unpaid balance" (in other words, the money remaining in the policy as level payments are made) over a *fixed term or period of 20 years.* Twenty years is Paul's approximate life expectancy.

This 20-year fixed-period payout contract provides Paul a level payment of $16,000 annually, starting on his 66th birthday. Payments would continue until his 85th year, for a total payout of $320,000—a tidy $120,000 profit. If Paul chooses this option, he may gain the benefit of asset protection (depending on the laws in his state) and he will definitely improve his cash flow. Remember the tax-deferral benefits of accumulation annuities? Well, the IRS also gives annuity *income* a break. It does this by "levelizing" the portion of each payment that is taxable. In this case, the IRS would exclude $10,000—1/20 of the original $200,000—annually from taxable income. This means Paul would only have to pay tax on $6,000 annually, instead of the full $16,000 payout. Assuming Paul is in a 30 percent tax bracket, he will pay $1,800 in taxes each year he receives a $16,000 payment. That will leave him with $14,200 annually ($16,000 to $1,800 in taxes), which is more than double the $7,000 Paul would net after paying taxes on earnings from a conventional savings plan that also pays 5 percent in interest earnings.

It's important to understand the key differences between unconventional savings instruments such as payout annuities and more traditional savings assets, such as CDs, treasuries, and bonds. Realize that extra cash flow from fixed period payout annuities comes with a price: Eventually, both principal and interest expire. When you withdraw interest only from CDs, treasuries, and bonds, you keep principal more or less intact. That's the main difference.

Payout Annuities Versus Conventional Savings Vehicles: What You'll Have 20 Years Later

	Original "Deposit"	Annual Payments, Pre-tax	Annual Net Payments After Taxes	20-Year Return
Fixed payout annuity, 5% interest on unpaid balance	$200,000	$16,000	$14,200	$284,000 ($14,200 in net payments × 20). No remaining principal
CD, 5% interest	$200,000	$10,000	$7,000	$140,000 in net interest earnings, plus $200,000 in intact principal
20 year treasury, 5% interest	$200,000	$10,000	$7,000	Same
Bond fund, 5% interest	$200,000	$10,000	$7,000	Principal may be more or less the same

Observations:

This chart presumes that 5 percent interest is payable with each alternative—a fixed period payout annuity (that credits interest on the annuity's unpaid balance), CD, treasury, or highly rated bond fund. Which actually pays the highest interest credits? This is a complicated question, and the answer will depend on bond yield curves.

As I write this in early 2010, annuity interest credits are the highest, CD interest rates the lowest. However, if all three alternatives credit 5 percent interest, they give the same mathematical result over a 20-year period. Go to Chart 1 on page 23 and Chart 2 on page 29 in chapter 1 to verify this.

This covers the basics of payout or income annuities, called SPIAs. As I showed you in the earlier example, Paul could obtain, say, a $200,000 fixed period SPIA contract. If it credits 5 percent interest on the unpaid balance, he'll receive a level annual payment of about $16,000—for a total of $320,000 over 20 years. This is not the only use for SPIAs. I'll cover other possibilities later on in this chapter.

Before I do that, however, let me acquaint you with one of the best ideas of all in retirement income planning. It combines a SPIA with an SPDA for some dazzling results. I call this strategy a "split savings plan."

A PAYOUT AND ACCUMULATION ANNUITY COMBINATION—A SPLIT SAVINGS PLAN

It isn't difficult to understand the traditional approach to living off money in retirement. Let's say Paul has $200,000 in an investment or savings vehicle that pays a 5 percent annual income of $10,000. Of course, he owes any taxes on his $10,000 payment. And he'll have his $200,000 in retirement income capital, plus or minus.

If Paul is willing to get a little more creative, he can get a superior result financially from a split savings plan. In this strategy, some capital is liquidated (annuitized) as another share is accumulated in an SPDA. It is much better taxwise than simply distributing taxable interest earned by a group of conventional savings vehicles. It may also afford a measure of asset protection, a subject discussed in detail in Appendix A.

Here is how the split savings plan could work for Paul, who wants a $10,000 income from his $200,000 in savings capital.

Paul takes that $200,000 and divides it into two portions: A (liquidation) and B (accumulation). Let's assume that annuities credit 5 percent interest, the same interest he would earn with a conventional savings plan. With portion A—$125,000—he acquires a 20-year fixed period level payout annuity. That gives him $10,000 annually, for a total of $200,000 over 20 years. (Over that period, he would use up that fund.)

Paul dedicates portion B—the remaining $75,000—to an SPDA. (Actually, portion B could go into most any vehicle that gives tax-deferred growth, including, say, a buy-and-hold stock, raw land, a mountain cabin, or cash value life insurance.) I use an SPDA here because it is free of management worries and clearly gives tax deferral over the 20-year-period. The idea is to use the 5 percent interest to build the fund back up to $200,000 in the 20th year, which would happen. Then Paul could divide his $200,000 SPDA once more into another SPIA/SPDA combination.

Before he does, however, he should ask a financial advisor to help him understand the "timing" issues that arise when an annuity (portion B) is exchanged for two new annuities. There can be tax issues here.

This split savings strategy confers three advantages:

First, Paul's portion A $10,000 annuity is income tax favored, with only $3,750 subject to taxes. That's much better than paying taxes on a full $10,000 in taxable interest, as he would if the $200,000 were invested in a conventional savings vehicle. (It's equivalent to getting a brand new income tax deduction of $6,250 each year for 20 years.)

Second, the $10,000 in annuity payments may enjoy asset protection, which is not afforded to conventional interest-only savings plans.

Third, if portion B ($75,000) can build back to $200,000 tax deferred, Paul defers taxes until he cashes in or systematically liquidates this fund at a later date. Neat trick, isn't it? That's almost like eating your cake and having it too! What a great way to build an income that keeps on going.

Doesn't that seem smarter than a conventional savings plan that merely credits interest on a sum of capital? Paul could always self-amortize that $125,000 (from the example), but he'd have to carefully manage the process to oversee idle funds and back-end surrender charges in CDs. A split savings approach that uses a payout annuity eliminates much of that hassle.

Realize, of course, that in a split savings plan, in this particular example, Paul would have to transfer $125,000 to an insurance company to obtain a $10,000 annual annuity income. To give Paul more control over his money, his payout annuity could give him a right to commute payments. (Just be aware: If annuity payments are protected from claimants in your state, commutation rights—which give you control over your money once more—could weaken this protection.) He could also maintain a sound line of credit for an emergency. Finally, he'll always have access to cash values in portion B if it is in an SPDA.

If you are in similar circumstances, a split savings plan may be a good option for you. A SPIA-SPDA combination is management free, convenient, tax advantaged, and—depending on the laws in your state—potentially protected from claimants. Compare these benefits to those available in a conventional savings programs, and you'll see that the split savings plan comes up a winner. Do realize, however, that the specific allocations used for liquidation and accumulation in the earlier example may not be in the right proportions for your individual circumstances. For best results, I'd take this idea to a financial advisor who knows your objectives.

LIFELONG PAYOUT ANNUITIES

In the previous situation, Paul wanted merely to receive $10,000 from his $200,000 in retirement income capital. We looked at a conventional savings plan. Then we compared that to a split savings plan that gave optimal results as $10,000 was paid to Paul each year from a $125,000 fixed period SPIA.

Now let's assume that Paul would like to derive maximum annuity income from his full $200,000. We'll look at what happens if all this money goes into fixed-level payments of $16,000 from a payout annuity that credits 5 percent interest on its unpaid balance within the contract. This time, there will be a twist. Paul's payout annuities will pay him for life—a life-only income, instead of payments for a set period certain of 20 years.

(In late 2009, a male, age 65, would receive about the same $16,000 annual amount from a $200,000 SPIA, whether it is a 20-year period certain or life-only contract. I'll assume this is what Paul receives from his life-only annuity.)

So now Paul receives a $16,000 payment each year for the rest of his life, whether he dies at age 66 or 106. (Should Paul live to merely life expectancy, let's say age 85, he'll receive $320,000 in payments—20 × $16,000.) If Paul waits until he is older to purchase that annuity, he'll receive an even larger payout for the same premium.

Here's why: the insurance company figures he has fewer years to live, so it is willing to increase the payout over the remaining years.

If Paul far outlives his life expectancy, a lifelong payout annuity could be a sweet deal. He could potentially receive far more in payouts than $320,000, bringing his overall interest credited return closer to, say, 7 or even 7¾ percent, for a completely safe investment. (For example, if $200,000 pays him $16,000 for 40 years—a total of $640,000—the interest rate earned on the unpaid balance would amount to nearly 7¾ percent per annum.)

THE "MATH" THAT ADDS UP TO 7¾ PERCENT INTEREST

Let me give you a little more detail on math that applies to income from a lifelong payout annuity. Say you have an amortization chart like Chart 3 in chapter 1 on page 35. It shows that $200,000 will pay a level $16,000 over 20 years if your unpaid balance credits 5 percent interest. (As I write this in November 2009, top-rated insurance carriers would pay about $15,000—something like 4¼ percent interest on the unpaid balance.) If it had a 40th year result, age 66 to 105, it would show that if that same $200,000 pays $16,000 over 40 years, you'll in effect earn 7⅝ percent interest on the unpaid balance.

But will you really? Where do these 5 percent and 7⅝ percent rates come from? Actually, they come from, say, some of the annuity owners of your same age and gender who bought the same policy—a policy that assures payments for life—and died early.

The bottom line: Lifelong payout annuities do well for those who live longer because these policies are credited with something from those who die earlier. If the insurance company guesses wrong about this, it pays out the difference. (And it must post reserves for shortfalls, under regulations by state insurance departments.)

On the other hand, if insurers guess right (and more people die than expected), they can't—under the rules—spend the windfall since they could be wrong next year.

That's why it appears you could earn nearly 7¾ percent interest if you live a long time. Some of this will come from a few folks who die early.

The longer the policyholder lives, the better a lifetime SPIA looks. Of course, Paul could die before he receives enough payments to break even. That would be unfortunate for his heirs, who might otherwise have received that money.

To mitigate that risk, Paul might consider:

1. A *life annuity with a term certain,* perhaps one that pays him for 20 years or life, *whichever period is longer.* Here he'd probably have to settle for a somewhat lower annual payout, perhaps $13,500 instead of the original $16,000. (The trade-off for a guaranteed minimum payout period is the lower payment.)

2. A *temporary life annuity due,* which could pay, say, $18,000 annually for 20 years or life, *whichever period is shorter.* This would give Paul even more cash flow.

3. *A lifelong SPIA with lesser term certains such as 5, 10, or 15 years.* For instance, if Paul's $200,000 life-only SPIA pays $16,000 annually, a lifetime annuity with a 5-year term-certain contract might pay $15,400 annually for at least the next 5 years. If Paul dies after getting only three $15,400 installments, his beneficiary would get the next two. Paul still has his lifetime guarantee. The longer the term certain, the less Paul would receive. A life annuity with a 10-year term certain might pay $14,800; one with a 15-year term certain might pay $14,200.

4. A "*cash or installment refund*" *SPIA,* which guarantees that the premium will always be returned. Here's how this works: Paul purchases a lifetime SPIA for $200,000. Without a guarantee, he might have received $16,000 in annual income, but *with this guarantee,* the amount drops to $15,000 annually. If Paul dies before he receives back a full $200,000 in payments, the beneficiary he designates gets the rest. If Paul were to receive $15,000 in payments for 10 years for a total of $150,000 before he died, his beneficiary would get the remaining $50,000, three payments of $15,000 each, plus $5,000. The beneficiary might also have the right to commute or accelerate these payments into a lump sum cash settlement.

5. A *joint and survivor annuity*, which would not only provide lifelong income for Paul, but also for a spouse, his child, or in fact, any person he names. Since there are two "lifetimes" in this contract, his payment will be less than $16,000. It all depends on the sex and age of the other individual.

DO SERIOUS HEALTH PROBLEMS RULE OUT SPIAS?

The short answer: not necessarily. You might think a life-only income annuity would be a bad deal for anyone with a chronic or serious health problem that could lead to an early death. However, some insurers will review an annuity applicant's health and increase income if there is a documented health condition.

For example let's say that Ted, age 65, has a medical history— perhaps he has had a stroke or a heart attack or is being treated for cancer—and his health makes it unlikely that he will even reach 85, which today is considered by the IRS a "normal" lifespan for someone age 65. Based on Ted's health condition, his life expectancy is likely to be age 78.

Ted applies for Company XYZ's $200,000 installment refund annuity where his annual payment is $15,000. (Let's say Ted dies in 10 years after receiving annual payments that total $150,000 each. Then his beneficiary receives $50,000 in payments over the next few years, bringing overall receipts to $200,000.)

Because of Ted's health condition (and his reduced life expectancy), Company XYZ increases his annual payment from $15,000 to $20,000. If Ted recovers and lives many more years despite his poor health, you can imagine what he'll receive from his $200,000 life annuity. Note that Ted (and his beneficiary) will still be guaranteed a total of $200,000 in payments.

Here is what you can expect in the near future: Carriers will get more comfortable with medically determined annuity payouts and develop new payout contracts. Consumers looking to life incomes will demand policies that adapt to all kinds of facts and circumstances. As a result of these related trends, look for carriers to become creative and provide more attractive SPIA features to consumers.

Additional Benefits of Payout Annuities

As I said earlier, it's especially wise to use lifelong payout annuities to generate a healthy portion of your retirement income. This is the only commercial financial product that's like Social Security; it can also provide retirement income up until death. In addition to providing a base pension, SPIAs—whether for life, a term certain, or both, confer a number of advantages. I've touched on these already, but let's look at them in greater detail.

SPIAs offer administrative ease

All SPIAs eliminate paperwork, files, and record keeping. There is no need to mull over brokerage reports, proxy statements, or 1099s. Once a year—at tax time—insurance companies provide all the information you'll need. When SPIA income is sent directly to a bank account, you can set up automatic bill payments directly from your bank account to your creditors. There are no more checks to write; past-due notices and late payment fees will naturally decrease.

SPIAs may have special asset protection features

With regard to the asset protection I explained in chapter 6, SPIAs can be especially advantageous. For instance, a number of states offer no safeguards for cash values in accumulation annuities (SPDAs). However, in those same states, there could be laws or court cases that provide full shelter for streams of income under a payout option. If SPIAs are of interest to you, review relevant laws in your state or engage a lawyer with expertise in asset protection-oriented estate planning to do it for you. You—or the lawyer—will need a copy of your state's debtor/creditor/annuity statutes.

Let's say, for example, that you and your advisors determine that you live in a state where income streams from SPIAs are afforded creditor protection. When you reach age 65, your advisors suggest that you deploy $100,000 cash (or cash in an SPDA) into a lifetime SPIA that pays $8,000 annually. The goal is to legitimately replace $100,000 (fully subject to claimants) with annual payments of $8,000 that are protected from creditors, lawsuits, and bankruptcy. At the time, there are no claims against you, and you have no reason to anticipate any. Still, you want the safeguards just in case.

It's hard to know whether a SPIA's income stream (once received) has state-specific, absolute, ongoing, and continuing asset protection in your state. If its cash flow is spent to support you and your family, it probably stands the best chance. Again, you or your advisor will need to check your state's debtor/creditor/annuity statutes.

SPIA incomes are tax favored

For scores of years, annuity incomes—even if paid over short periods such as 5 years—have been tax favored in our system. By tax favored, I again refer to the levelizing of that portion of each payment that is taxable. Here is an example: A $100,000 SPIA pays $8,000 annually at the end of the year for a 20-year period—a total payout of $160,000. Taxes would be assessed on the following basis: The $100,000 "investment in the contract" would be considered the numerator in a fraction, and $160,000 (the anticipated return) would be the denominator. Therefore, 62.5 percent ($100,000 ÷ $160,000) of each payment would be excluded from taxes; 37.5 percent would be included as taxable income.

This is quite different from self-amortizing $100,000 over a period of 20 years. Here, most of the first year's payment is taxable, and virtually all of the last year's payment is tax free. This "debt repayment" approach to spending money heaps taxes early—a more costly tax result than annuitizing with a SPIA.

SPIA incomes have an edge over guaranteed lifetime withdrawal benefits (GLWBs)

Let's say you own an SPDA. Now, you are ready to take out income—a switch to a SPIA or a withdrawal plan, a GLWB. There is debate about whether SPIAs (which amortize money) are better than Guaranteed Lifetime Withdrawal Benefits (GLWBs), which give policyholders rights to simply take out money from special lifetime withdrawal "accounts" and allow guaranteed withdrawals at a specific rate. For instance, a GLWB in a variable annuity contract might permit a withdrawal of 5 to 6 percent when the policyholder reaches age 60, 6 to 7 percent when she begins payments in her 70s, and 7 to 8 percent if she begins payments in her 80s.

The withdrawal percentage might be applied to the *higher* of the contract's actual accumulation value, or the contract's lifetime withdrawal account. Even if a variable annuity declines in value, the withdrawal rate may be applied to locked-in profits. Let's say there is a 6.5 percent withdrawal right. It pays $6,500 annually from an SPDA's $100,000 lifetime withdrawal account value. As applied to the accumulation account, it might look this way. (See below, "An SPDA's Withdrawals from a $100,000 Lifetime Withdrawal Account.") Notice in the chart that as the accumulation account increases (from $90,000 to $120,000) in Year 2, the amount withdrawn increases as well (from $6,500 to $7,800). In this SPDA, the increase is locked in and remains level until another increase in the accumulation account's value.

An SPDA's Withdrawals from a $100,000 Lifetime Withdrawal Account

Year	Accumulation Account Value	A 6.5% Withdrawal Rate on a Contract's Accumulation Account
1	$90,000	$6,500
2	$120,000	$7,800
3	$80,000	$7,800

While the withdrawal rate of 6.5 percent in this example is fixed and guaranteed by the company, your accumulation value is not. This is why this contract is called a variable annuity and can produce substantially lower cash surrender values.

In general, I still think SPIAs have the edge here. A well-conceived lifelong SPIA plan has levelized taxation, rights of commutation, and side fund emergency money "outside" the SPIA.

(SPIAs may have more creditor protection than GLWBs as well.) Actually, fixed SPIAs give a predictable base income, which may possibly allow a more aggressive investment strategy for other assets.

Nonetheless, GLWBs do assure withdrawals and are attractive compared with SPIAs that assign capital without policyowner access. If the SPDA has earned high-interest credits (fixed-indexed policies) or upside (as with variable annuities), a SPIA payout will probably be better. If there have been low-interest credits or low-variable annuity performance, GLWB payments directly from the withdrawal account may be better.

Just be aware that you can't access an SPDA's "capital" in a guaranteed lifetime withdrawal account. It is only there for the calculation of an amount that can be taken from the contract.

A word of caution: When compared to SPIAs, GLWBs (which assure withdrawals from a hypothetical account) are somewhat untested. Could some GLWBs promise more than they can deliver? And will GLWB withdrawals in your state be more available to third-party claimants—creditors, ex-spouses, and others? As methods of liquidating capital, either GLWBs or SPIAs, or both, are helpful. Bring up your questions with your financial advisor.

HOW TO REPLACE INCOME AFTER A STOCK MARKET CRASH

Let's say you had $100,000 invested (before the 2008 and 2009 stock market meltdown) that generated 5 percent interest ($5,000) on your money. Here's the capital you'll need now to have the same $5,000 in lifetime income from a fixed SPIA.

Note: Compared with the pre-meltdown income, your annuity base will be tax favored, and it may be protected from claimants. These are additional reasons to consider the SPIA.

Male Age	Pre-Meltdown Asset Base	Asset Base Annual Income at 5%	Single Premium Immediate Life Annuity *	Annual Annuity Income
85	$100,000	$5,000	$28,500	$5,000
80	$100,000	$5,000	$35,500	$5,000
75	$100,000	$5,000	$44,000	$5,000
70	$100,000	$5,000	$52,000	$5,000
65	$100,000	$5,000	$59,000	$5,000

*Sample annuity premium rates for a $5,000 annual income—mid-2009.

A SPIA to replace income from lost capital—what a great idea! Know, also, that this chart can be used to compare a $250,000 CD that pays $5,000 or so in annual income. If you are age 65, a SPIA that pays $5,000 but costs only $59,000 is an attractive alternative. You'll even have $191,000 ($250,000–$59,000) remaining from the CD to invest, generate more income, purchase long-term care insurance, or have some fun.

THE RIGHT TO "COMMUTE" OR ACCELERATE PAYMENTS

Of course, SPIAs have drawbacks as well. Some criticize SPIAs because of the seeming loss of control over the single premium. Nowadays, you can have a right to commute that allows access to what remains in your annuity. Essentially, this is a right to accelerate any remaining payments, converting them once more into a lump sum.

Here is an example of commutation: For $100,000, you obtain a SPIA that pays $8,000 annually at the end of the year for 20 years. After 1 year, you want your money back. An insurer calculates a "present value" of the future income stream at, say, $94,000 (a figure I've estimated just for the purpose of this example). According to the contract, you can always have this sum after a surrender charge of 6 percent. Here, you can cash out (or commute) for

$88,360 (94 percent × $94,000). At least you'll get access to most of your money.

The idea of commuting or accelerating annuity payments to "liquefy" SPIAs is becoming popular. In a 2007 survey by Milliman, an actuarial consulting firm, 14 of 25 insurers surveyed say they allow commutation of future income from a SPIA. (Again, this weakens any asset protection offered to SPIAs without such features.)

Another Way to Protect Against "Living too Long"

Perhaps you feel that cash outs (commutation, acceleration, etc.) seem like too much to bear. You understand longevity risks associated with living longer and running out of money, yet you don't want to commit your capital to an annuity carrier. Perhaps you feel that you can do an adequate job managing your retirement finances on your own, at age 60 or 65. You prefer to make investment decisions and capital allocations based on your investment experience and current income needs. At the same time, you are a little unsure about the "end game"—that time toward the end of your life expectancy (after age 80) when you just can't be certain about the outcome you might actually achieve over the intervening 20 to 25 years or so. (All you have to do is pick up the local paper to imagine that the individuals in the paper are you!) During this time, you are probably too old to make significant financial recoveries.

There's still a way to hedge your bets and protect against "living too long." It's called longevity insurance and it works like this: Let's say that you turn 65, and your circumstances are such that you *could* use $100,000 to acquire a SPIA that pays $8,000 annually for 20 years. (This seems better than a lifelong SPIA where payments cease at an early death.) You are still concerned about losing control of your money and running out of income if you live past 85, when the 20 years of payouts would come to an end.

Voila! For merely a one-time, nonrefundable $10,000 premium, XYZ Insurance Company promises a lifelong income security blanket of $8,000 *beginning at age 85.* In other words, you solve the longevity risk at a cost of only $10,000. Once this premium is paid, you'll have $90,000 remaining to save or invest for income during the next 20 years. You'll always have $8,000 in SPIA income coming, but only if you attain age 85. In essence, you've hedged things. You have full control of $90,000, which is most of your money. But you also guarantee a lifelong income of $8,000 (if you are still alive at age 85). Of course, if you have a stroke or mismanage money in the meantime, you may have to eat cat food and drink cheap beer until you reach 85, when your income will be restored. Let's hope that doesn't occur at age 84 or, God forbid, earlier!

A VARIANT—SINGLE PREMIUM DEFERRED IMMEDIATE ANNUITIES

Up until now, I have referred to annuities as either accumulation or payout. But there is a form that bridges both—I call it a *single premium deferred immediate annuity* (or SPDIA). It acts like an accumulation annuity in the build-up phrase (but there is no cash surrender value). It becomes an immediate annuity during the payout phase.

The SPDIA just might be a great idea—the planning tool of choice for a young saver who would like to convert a nice bonus, a sizable money gift, or an inheritance into an annuity that should guarantee a specific income later when that individual reaches age 65 or 70.

Let's say Jean, age 45, uses a $100,000 windfall to purchase a deferred immediate fixed annual annuity that should guarantee about $22,000 annually some 21 years later when she turns 66. Once Jean hits that birthday, she'll receive a lifelong income and a minimum of 10 payments. This plan assures that she will receive, at the very least, a minimum payout of $220,000 ($22,000 × 10 payments). She could receive as much as $440,000 total if she lives 20 years to age 85 (her IRS life expectancy) and even more than that if she lives into her 90s or beyond. That's more than a four-fold increase—without taking any risks. From Jean's 45th year until her 66th year, the money would build in a safe, secure, tax-deferred annuity contract. It's possible the money could be protected from creditors as well, depending on the laws in the state where Jean lives.

A younger individual who can afford to set aside that money for even longer could get an even more startling result.

Sound good?

The downside, of course, is that Jean won't have that $100,000 for the 21 years if she purchases this kind of contract. And, should she die before she reaches age 65, her beneficiary might receive merely $100,000 in installments. Her beneficiary might even have to wait until Jean would have turned 65 to receive the full sum, or settle with the insurer for a lesser income that could begin immediately. (All of this will be spelled out in the contract, which should be read carefully.)

Personally, I think it is smart to purchase these units of deferred income (and simply forget about it). But keep in mind—unless there is a right to commute, there is no access to your capital ever. Nonetheless, deferred incomes have a "present value" that can be on a financial statement. You might even persuade a commercial lender to advance capital against this expected income too. (A word of caution: if the annuity contract is pledged for such a loan, it could cause current taxes on any profit accumulated in your annuity contract.)

The other advantages of a SPDIA are the tax-deferred interest credits on your $100,000 premium and any asset protection available under your state laws. Since your insurer can invest your money long term, it will likely credit very competitive rates on your money. This will be reflected in the amount of income when it begins. (If your deferred immediate annuity contract contains mortality-based payments—a life contingency—see the prior discussion on page 140 regarding mortality in "The 'Math' That Adds Up to 7¾ Percent Interest.")

As of 2010, there are just a few deferred immediate annuities on the market. Since these vary a great deal, you'll want to shop wisely and read the contract carefully prior to making a purchase.

ANNUITIES: A BRIEF ASSET PROTECTION ANALYSIS

Although annuities are at least partially protected from claimants in about two-thirds of the states, they don't enjoy as much safeguarding as life insurance. *Here's why*: Annuities are more aligned with retirement income and pension planning; life insurance is associated with responsibility to support family. Presumably, the former is less significant to society than the latter.

Nonetheless, a number of states do shelter annuity cash values and death proceeds. Florida, for example, has no limitation on its exemption of annuity values. Roughly 35 states have complete or nearly complete protection for cash values and death proceeds. (See "A State-by-State Look" on page 229.) Protection may be better for offshore annuities, but these aren't subject to U.S. state insurance department rules and regulations. There may also be more creative investments for funds in these policies. The tradeoff here is no U.S. protection from the SEC.

Creditor protection for annuities is similar to the shelter afforded life insurance. You need to know who and how much is safe from whose creditors. Get answers to these six questions:

1. Is an annuity beneficiary's death benefit shielded from his or her creditors or creditors of the policyowner, or annuitant? (An annuitant is a person whose life expectancy is used to measure payments from a payout annuity. He or she could be the policyowner or another person.)

2. Is there protection if premiums are paid with intent to hinder, delay, or defraud creditors?

3. Are cash values safeguarded? Is income from a payout contract protected?

4. Does shelter depend on a beneficiary's relationship to the policyowner?

5. Are annuity proceeds still sheltered when they reach your bank—even when they are reinvested?

6. Finally, are prearranged beneficiary settlement option agreements favored under your state's law? I'll discuss settlement options more fully in chapter 10.

As you'll discover, there are subtleties in the laws. You'll find that some states:

- protect the contract—no matter the parties (policyowner, annuitant, and beneficiary), and other state laws mention which party is protected;

- give more protection if an annuity payee is dependent on the policyowner-debtor for financial support (an annuity payee is someone who receives payments from a payout annuity);

- safeguard lottery annuity winnings, no less;

- shelter private annuities between individuals, and charitable gift annuities as well as commercial contracts;
- shield a contract where acquired, even though the policy-owner lives elsewhere;
- shield contract values if you establish residence there after acquiring an annuity in another state; and
- have vague and poorly written protective statutes.

As with life insurance, you can't pay annuity premiums to defraud creditors. But it may be difficult to show intent to defraud when conventional assets and cash are converted to annuities. Annuities are usually purchased for an income in retirement and not to deceive anyone.

In summary, there is significant protection for annuities. But, if there is more shelter for insurance values in your state, look carefully at which savings vehicle is better for you. This might even color your thinking about where to live in retirement.

IF SPIAS ARE SO GREAT, WHY DO THEY HAVE SUCH A SMALL MARKET SHARE?

As I said in the last chapter, SPIAs represent only 2 to 3 percent of the annuity market—despite their great value. Insurers haven't done much when it comes to payout annuities that systematically liquidate capital. There are several reasons why.

One is that the mainstream media and money managers are more comfortable thinking about investment accumulation. Many financial services professionals would rather receive an annual fee on a growing portfolio under annual withdrawals than a one-time commission on money that is being liquidated via an irrevocable payment annuity.

It is also to an insurance agent's advantage to promote the transfer of money in one SPDA into a new insurer's SPDA contract, tax free, because the transaction to do so pays a commission. Once SPDAs are converted into SPIAs, there are no more exchange opportunities and, usually, no more sales commissions for the selling agent.

Another problem is the carrier themselves. Many are not too anxious to assume such long-term commitments with guarantees they may not be able or wish to support for future years. It's easier and less risky with more near-term profitability for them to offer different flavored withdrawal options and just let the consumer worry about how long the money will last.

That covers the basics of SPIAs and a variation, the SPDIA, two exceedingly useful financial instruments for anyone crafting a retirement income plan. Let's turn our attention in the next chapter to the third planning cornerstone, Individual Retirement Accounts.

IRAs AND QPs: BASIC AND ADVANCED STRATEGIES

The Individual Retirement Account brings together two
tremendously powerful forces, both of which benefit you:
1) compound interest and 2) tax savings.
—David Wolpe

The name says it all: Individual Retirement Account (IRA). This is
a category of personal retirement savings plans available to individuals who earn taxable compensation—bonuses, commissions, fees,
salaries, separate maintenance payments, taxable alimony, tips, and
wages. Actually, there are eleven types of IRAs, but we'll focus on
only two in this chapter—the traditional and the Roth IRA.

These tax-favored plans offer strong creditor protection, two
good reasons to add an IRA—if you don't already have one—to
your retirement portfolio. (See "IRAs/QPs: A Brief Asset Protection Analysis," on page 177.) Consider an IRA, as well, if you have
funds to "roll over" from a 401(k) or employer pension account.
Traditional IRAs—smartly combined with other savings vehicles
such as single premium deferred annuities and life insurance—can

truly magnify your retirement income. So can Roth IRAs, which can work tax magic long after you reach retirement age.

Keep in mind, of course, that you don't want just an IRA—you also want to employ annuities, cash value life insurance, and your home as part of your quality lifelong retirement income program.

A word of caution: IRA rules can be difficult to understand. But understand them you must. Otherwise you can lose money unnecessarily to penalties or taxes. To help you avoid this, I have made every effort to explain the rules clearly. Please read this chapter carefully—and then review it a second or third time so you not only understand the rules, but will also remember them.

SOME BACKGROUND

Here are some interesting facts, according to the Investment Company Institute (www.ici.org). IRAs comprise the single largest component of the U.S. retirement market. (On December 31, 2008, they accounted for $3.6 trillion in assets.) Currently, more than two households in every five have at least one IRA. Most people have traditional IRAs; less than 5 percent of IRA assets are in Roth IRAs.

IRAs began as part of a comprehensive Employee Retirement Security Act of 1974 (ERISA). Initially, workers could make tax-deductible cash contributions of 15 percent of compensation, up to a maximum of $1,500 annually. There were 6 percent penalty taxes (on any excess) if contributions exceeded the limit, and a 10 percent penalty for taxable distributions before age 59½. There was also a 50 percent penalty when an IRA owner failed to take specified minimum withdrawals after age 70½, a penalty still in force for traditional IRAs, although not Roth IRAs.

Some rules have changed over the years. As a result, you can now make an IRA contribution of 100 percent of compensation, up to $5,000 yearly, plus an extra $1,000 "catch-up" amount if you are age 50 or older.

The 1974 legislation established the so-called "traditional" IRA. A newer form of IRA—named the Roth after its legislative sponsor, the late Senator William Roth of Delaware—was established by the Taxpayer Relief Act of 1997. It became effective for tax year 1998.

There are distinct differences between the two, which I will detail next. In brief, however, a traditional IRA benefits account owners by allowing tax deferral on IRA contributions—until the account owner reaches age 70½. The thinking is that owners will be in a lower tax bracket when they withdraw principal and interest from the account, which is when taxes come due.

Let's say, for instance, that Sally contributes $5,000 of her $50,000 in annual income to a traditional IRA (but not a Roth IRA) this year. She will only pay taxes on $45,000, deferring the taxes on the deductible $5,000 IRA contribution and any earnings that accumulate, until she withdraws the funds. This can lower her overall tax payments if she is, indeed, in a lower tax bracket when she retires and takes the money out.

After age 70½, the owner of a traditional IRA (but not a Roth IRA) will have to take *required minimum distributions* (RMDs) under a special IRS Table, whether the owner needs the money or not. This forces money out of the account, and again, taxes become due.

A Roth IRA has similar contribution limits, but the tax structure is different. You have to pay the tax on the earnings you contribute, but once the money is in the Roth, it will build tax *free*. If you follow all of the rules, you won't *ever* have to pay taxes on withdrawals. Roths are especially attractive if you'll be in a higher tax bracket during retirement.

For certain kinds of savers, this is an exceedingly good deal since compound interest in a tax free environment can add so much more to the account than the tax-paid dollars initially contributed. Because there is no requirement for withdrawals at age 70½, assets in a Roth IRA can grow tax free for a much longer period than in a traditional IRA. Paying taxes on earnings contributed to a Roth may also work out better for individuals who are much more comfortable saving money when they know they and their beneficiaries won't have to pay any taxes on earnings—ever.

Let's look at the principal features of each IRA in more detail.

TRADITIONAL IRAS

The cash amount you can contribute each year is limited by the *lesser* of your earned compensation, or $5,000 for those under age 50, and $6,000 for those age 50 or older. For instance, if Ben only earns $1,500 a year, he may not deduct more than $1,500 contributed to his IRA. If Ben is married, however, and his wife earns at least $8,500, she can contribute $5,000 to her IRA and $3,500 for Ben—and take a tax deduction on the full $8,500. In other words, a married couple filing a joint return and earning compensation of at least $10,000 can contribute all of it to two IRAs—$5,000 for each spouse. And, they could even use cash in a $10,000 savings account for the contributions.

Know that if you participate in a qualified 401(k) plan at work or have an employer-sponsored pension (QP), there will be limitations on how much of your allowable IRA contributions you can deduct from your taxes. In 2010, for instance, if you are single, an "active participant" in a QP, and have an adjusted gross income (AGI) of $66,000 or above (or if you are married, "active participants," and file a joint return with an AGI of $109,000 or above), you can't deduct anything—the IRA deduction is zero! You can still make a nondeductible contribution, however, up to $5,000 (or $6,000 if you are age 50 before the end of the year) and still benefit from tax deferral on growth.

Contributions made to traditional IRAs can be used to purchase a variety of investments, such as stocks, bonds, certificates of deposit, and so on. Banks have IRA plans for CDs; insurers have annuity plans called IRANS; securities people have stocks and mutual funds; and some trust companies have what are called "self-directed accounts," where a trustee allows an IRA owner to choose the IRA's investments. (I will talk more about these later.) However, an IRA cannot invest in life insurance or directly in art, stamps, antiques, or gems. Neither can an account borrow money or be security for a loan.

Again, the advantage of a traditional IRA is immediate tax savings. Let's say you are in a 25 percent tax bracket and you contribute $4,000 this year. That will net you $1,000 in immediate tax savings, which you could save or invest.

While the money remains in a traditional IRA, direct contributions, plus any interest, dividends, or capital gains, build tax free. But you don't get a free ride forever. Again, when you reach age 70½, special RMD rules will force you to withdraw at least a small portion of the money in the account. Fortunately, RMDs aren't too painful taxwise. That first year, you'll take nearly 4 percent of the account's value. The percentage will increase gradually, to about 8 percent at, say, age 88 (and to a greater percentage thereafter). Since the percentages really aren't that large, many IRA owners should earn more than they withdraw over the years and die with considerably larger accounts than they had at age 70½.

Again, all distributions (except nondeductible contributions, if any) are taxable. If you planned well, however, you'll be in a lower tax bracket when you withdraw than you were when you put the money into your traditional IRA.

Here's the reason behind the RMD rules, which have been in effect since 1974: The government doesn't want you to accumulate in retirement accounts, defer taxes on earnings for decades on end, and then pass the untaxed money onto your beneficiaries. RMD rules force you to pay at least a portion of the taxes on that money during your lifetime, and require the same of your beneficiaries once the money passes to them. This puts the tax dollars back into circulation. The IRS gets its taxes one way or another.

You don't have to wait until you are age 70½ for access to your money, however. Distributions can begin anytime. But distributions taken before you turn age 59½ may be subject to a 10 percent penalty in addition to taxes due on the amount withdrawn. (There are exceptions, but I won't cover them here.) Once you reach 59½, you can take distributions without having to pay penalties. At that point, any such payments are considered part of your taxable income. If you need money up to age 70½, take it from savings that you have already paid taxes on and keep the IRA intact until you reach 70½. This will allow income to build in a tax-deferred account for as long as possible.

Advanced Planning Concepts with Traditional IRAs

What if you don't need income from your traditional IRA when you are age 70½? A friend of mine found himself in just this position. He had $250,000 in a traditional IRA, and another $250,000 in non-IRA investments that paid him more than enough income. Since he didn't need the money from his IRA, he hated the thought of paying taxes on a forced distribution. Was there *anything* he could do to lower his tax bill?

I told him the same thing I recommend to you should you find yourself in similar circumstances. If you don't need the income from personal investments, park it in a single premium deferred annuity (SPDA—see chapter 6), where it can build tax deferred over many years. My friend did this—and it was like flicking a switch. Before age 70½, he had to pay taxes on income from his personal investments. Then he put that money into an SPDA and bingo—no more current taxes on personal investment income. Now he simply pays taxes on RMDs from his IRA.

You might use funds in a traditional IRA to pay estimated income taxes. Let's say you pay $10,000 in quarterly estimated taxes. Instead of making these payments, you "withdraw" $40,000 from your IRA late this year. But don't take any cash; instead, have your IRA's custodian send the full $40,000 directly toward the tax estimate. The money will be treated as if it were your unpaid estimated taxes.

Then you repay the IRA within 60 days of receipt. Voila! You will have use of the government's money for a few months.

With this maneuver, the objective is to earn tax-deferred interest on much of the money you'd pay in four estimated tax installments. I first became acquainted with this concept when I read David B. Kearns's "Painless Tax Deferment," *Trusts and Estates* magazine, November 2003. I recommend the article to you and your tax preparer.

ROTH IRAS

As I said earlier, a Roth IRA is an IRA funded with after-tax dollars. Assets in the account can build tax deferred. Distributions—contributions and earnings—can be taken entirely tax and penalty free if the following *two* conditions are met:

1. More than 5 years have passed since you established the account. (The 5-year period begins January 1 of the first calendar year in which you first made a Roth contribution.)

2. You, the Roth IRA owner, are at least 59½ or you are disabled or meet certain qualifications such as being a "first-time" home buyer. (The IRS defines this as someone who has had no financial interest in a principal residence for at least 2 years prior to the purchase of the new home. Qualifying Roth home buyers can withdraw up to a lifetime limit of $10,000—tax free—for this purpose.) Or, you are the beneficiary and the account owner has died.

Both conditions must be met. If they aren't, you may have to pay income taxes and a 10 percent penalty tax on Roth earnings. Fortunately, distributions are deemed first from tax-paid principal, then your earnings. The rules can be difficult. If you have a Roth, consult your tax preparer before taking a lot of money from the account.

Investment opportunities and contributions limits are much the same as with a traditional IRA. If you make too much income in any given year, you won't be able to contribute to a Roth IRA. In 2010, if you file a tax return as an individual and have adjusted gross income (AGI) of $120,000 or more, or if you file jointly as a couple and have AGI of at least $177,000, you do not even qualify for a Roth contribution.

That said, there are probably fewer restrictions with a Roth, primarily because the government has already received its tax dollars on the earnings you've used to fund it.

With a Roth, as I said earlier, you can withdraw amounts of principal at any time without incurring penalties, as long as you follow the rules. If you have taxable compensation past age 70½, you can continue making contributions to the account. And you won't be required to take RMDs at age 70½ or beyond. In fact, the RMD rules won't come into play until the account passes to your beneficiaries.

A Roth IRA for a Grandchild

Here's a great gift idea to help an enterprising teenager.

Let's say your granddaughter, Tori, age 13, can earn $5,000 annually during her teens doing babysitting and odd jobs. You want to create a tax-favored and creditor-protected fund for her retirement.

You can do this—thanks to the Uniform Gift to Minors Act (UGMA).

Create a Roth IRA for Tori, putting it under her mother's or father's name, in accordance with the UGMA rules in the state where she lives. You'll match her $5,000 in earnings and contribute $5,000 annually for, say, 7 years to her Roth account. The account will be turned over to Tori officially in the year she becomes an adult, as defined under her state's law.

Here are the results, assuming a sustainable 5 percent rate of return:

- When Tori is 20, her IRA will be worth $42,750. (See Chart 2 in chapter 1, on page 29.)
- When Tori is 60, she'll own an account worth $300,892; at age 70, she'll have $489,905. (If you can achieve aggressive 8 percent returns throughout, Tori's IRA will be valued at $48,185 at age 20, and she'll be a Roth IRA millionaire at age 60.) Everything she withdraws then will be tax free. What a legacy for Tori, especially if income tax rates are higher in the future!
- Know also that your granddaughter's Roth IRA balance will be protected in the event of her bankruptcy at any time. If she

loses a lawsuit or has a creditor problem outside of bankruptcy, she'll probably have protection under her state's law as well.

- All this because of Tori's $5,000 in annual earnings and your seven annual $5,000 Roth IRA contributions for her!

As good as this Roth IRA idea seems, there might be something better. Stay with me.

You acquire a cash value life insurance contract on Tori's life. Assume that a $5,000 annual premium purchases a $300,000 Face Amount contract. (Actually, there is no $5,000 premium limit as with a Roth IRA, so you could buy even more life insurance if you wanted to.) The contract's cash value buildup is tax free, as long as money stays in the policy. Later, tax free withdrawals and loans are possible. Finally (if this concerns you), you won't have to put the policy in Tori's name when she becomes an adult. Another difference from the IRA under UGMA rules: you or her parents could wait to give the policy to her at age 40, for example. You wouldn't be required to give it to her as soon as she becomes an "adult" as determined by the state's UGMA rules.

Her life insurance cash values may be protected from creditors under state law, as with the IRA. Finally, the contract's death benefit (perhaps millions someday) will be available at Tori's death for her spouse, children, or charity. And everything can be tax free, as well.

SELF-DIRECTED IRAS

You can manage either a traditional or Roth IRA as a "self-directed IRA." This simply means that you retain the authority to choose your investments, instead of leaving the management to your broker or other financial professional. Here's the other perk: a self-directed account expands the range of investment options permitted by the IRS.

With a self-directed IRA, there are risks and rewards. A self-directed IRA must have a custodian—typically a bank or trust company—who takes care of administering the account. But you assume responsibility for the investment choices and pay fees for any special IRA services.

These accounts are designed for those who can access unique and nonmainstream investments in a tax-favored savings environment. For instance, a self-directed IRA might acquire:

- real estate, probably unimproved land such as a corner lot, and even depressed property in foreclosure;
- certain gold, silver, or platinum bullion that remains in the IRA trustee's possession; and
- timeshares, options/futures, foreign currency, mortgages—virtually any investment out of the mainstream, meaning something not typically offered by a securities firm, bank, or insurance company.

There are many ways to be creative with a self-directed traditional IRA. This strategy is one of my favorites. It uses a two-directional split similar to the one employed in chapter 7 on advanced annuity strategies, in which one fund is designed to grow so it could replenish the other fund, used for ongoing income.

You can do something similar with money in a self-directed IRA. Here's how.

Ned, age 70, wants to "fully" manage his $500,000 traditional IRA. He's high on the idea of switching to a self-directed account and wants to commit to long-term investments. He likes the freedom that would give him to include raw land, commodities, precious metals, and other good long-term bets in a self-directed account.

His biggest question: how to most effectively manage RMDs that he must take after age 70½. At that age, he'll have to withdraw nearly 4 percent ($20,000), an amount that will probably increase gradually over the years.

Here's what I suggest:

"Consider dividing the account into two portions: portion A and portion B," I say. "Portion A could be a $200,000 payout annuity that pays estimated RMDs on the *entire* IRA for 10 to 15 years." (An entire IRA would include the value of the account's investments and commutable payments in the payout annuity.) "Portion B—$300,000—might be fully invested. The result could be RMDs—personal income now from portion A, and growth from portion B for a new income plan in 10 to 15 years." This is another example of a split-savings plan where some money is liquidated and the balance is accumulated.

A ROTH OR A TRADITIONAL IRA: WHICH IS BEST FOR YOU?

At the risk of sounding evasive, only your financial planner—applying your answers to questions posed by special computerized IRA "calculators"—can say for sure. There are a number of variables that need to be taken into account, not all of them financial. The object, of course, is to determine which IRA will give you the greatest tax savings over time.

In general, however, Roths may be the better savings vehicle for many of those who meet the income limits because the potential for tax savings over time is much greater. The account can even be transferred to beneficiaries income tax free.

A Comparison of IRAs in 2009

	Traditional	**Roth**
1. How much can I contribute annually?	$5,000	$5,000
2. Are there additional catch-up amounts?	Yes! $1,000 if over age 50	Same
3. Can I earn too much to make a contribution?	No! But if you are an "active participant" in a qualified plan (QP) at work, your deduction may be limited based on AGI.	Yes—if AGI is over $120,000 for a single taxpayer, and if AGI is over $177,000 for a married taxpayer
4. Is there a maximum contribution age?	Yes! Age 70½ in tax year	
5. Can I deduct my contributions?	Yes! Unless limited—see 3 above	No
6. Can I contribute for my nonworking spouse?	Yes! You may contribute and deduct up to $5,000 for each, plus $1,000 if combined earnings are $10,000 ($12,000).	Yes, as long as your combined earnings are $10,000 ($12,000)
7. Is there a 10 percent penalty for taking out money pre-age 59½?	Yes, but there are exceptions to this rule.	Same
8. Must I take required minimum distributions (RMDs) at age 70½?	Yes	No
9. May I roll over 401(k) or QP money to my IRA?	Yes, and your spouse beneficiary (only) can too	Same
10. Can I convert my traditional account to a Roth?	Yes, and your spouse beneficiary can too	
11. Are my withdrawals and distributions taxable?	Generally yes	Generally no

Also, speaking only in the most general terms, the Roth IRA may be better for individuals who (a) have money outside the IRA to pay taxes now, (b) anticipate being in a *higher* tax bracket after they retire, (c) won't need IRA income after age 70½, or (d) want to save in a purely tax free environment.

For those of you over age 70½, the Roth offers these additional advantages over the traditional IRA:

- If you earn compensation after that age, you can still contribute to a Roth IRA. You can't do that with a traditional IRA.

- If a spouse is beneficiary, he or she can roll over the account and become the owner of the Roth IRA. If your spouse doesn't need the money, it can continue to build tax free in the account since there are no RMDs. If that spouse remarries and dies, his or her new spouse-beneficiary can roll over the account as well. (It's only when a nonspouse beneficiary inherits either traditional IRAs or Roths that RMDs are required.)

It doesn't get much better than that!

Be aware: When a nonspouse beneficiary receives the Roth, it must remain titled in the former account owner's name. For example, it might be titled, "Mary Jones, [former] IRA owner, FBO [for benefit of] my children equally." Then, Mary's children will take (tax free) RMDs over their lifetimes with tax free interest earned inside the account.

CONVERTING FROM A TRADITIONAL TO A ROTH IRA

If you are a high income earner, you could believe that tax rates are about to increase. You may be thinking about converting a traditional IRA to a Roth. If so, you just got lucky. Beginning in 2010, you can have unlimited AGI, convert to a Roth, and spread taxes pro rata during 2011 and 2012. Before then, a conversion was only available to those with an AGI of $100,000 or less.

The other requirement: You have to be the account owner or the spouse beneficiary who has assumed control of the account. (If you are the account owner and you want your spouse-beneficiary to have the ability to make the conversion, the beneficiary form must give him or her unrestricted rights to use the account.) Let's say you meet the requirements. Now what?

One strategy you can use is to switch the account in stages, instead of doing it all in 1 year. For example, a $300,000 traditional IRA could be converted roughly in $50,000 annual installments over 6 years. This might help you take advantage of a series of lower tax brackets.

Either way, I urge you to pay the tax money using a source outside of your IRA. The reason is that earlier you were probably paying taxes on its income. After eliminating the (taxable) tax fund, you've actually "switched" its income to "tax free" inside the Roth. Let me give an example.

Let's say Lois, age 60, has a $500,000 traditional Roth IRA. She also has a $150,000 personal CD that earns 5 percent ($7,500) annually. She's in a 30 percent tax bracket, and the earnings from her CD are taxable. To change that income from taxable to tax free, Lois uses the $150,000 CD for taxes and makes a Roth conversion. Now, she withdraws $7,500 from her $500,000 Roth IRA. Voila! Those earnings are no longer taxable!

Of course, Lois spent $150,000 in CD capital to get tax free earnings from the Roth. As I'll explain shortly, however, her net worth really hasn't changed. But now she's in a better position to build wealth. That $500,000 Roth can accumulate tax free interest for her as long as she wants. Provided she follows the rules, there won't be any taxes to pay on withdrawals from the account; Lois can always take tax free distributions. But she doesn't have to withdraw anything if she doesn't want to. She can now treat her IRA as a "government approved tax shelter" that builds its earnings tax free "forever."

Here's another example. This one involves a married couple. Fred, age 65, and Margie, age 60, have done a good job putting money away. Fred's traditional IRA, which he has built over 35 years, is worth about $200,000. Fred also has a $200,000 401(k) account in a plan that lets him roll that money over into an IRA. Margie, meanwhile, has a $100,000 IRA and $50,000 in her company's pension plan.

Fred and Margie could start Roths with annual contributions up to $6,000 each. Of course, they'd have to pay the taxes first if they take the money from Fred's traditional IRA and "convert" $6,000 of it into his Roth.

Let's say Fred has his 401(k) account transferred to a Roth. Here's how this would work.

Following the rules, Fred has the trustee of his $200,000 401(k) account roll its funds over to his new IRA. Then he converts the IRA to a Roth by including $200,000 in taxable income. The taxes are, say, $60,000, which are paid with a non-IRA savings account. Before the conversion, Fred owned (a) a $200,000 taxable 401(k) worth $140,000 after taxes and a $60,000 tax-paid savings account. After the conversion, he owns (b) merely a $200,000 tax-paid Roth IRA. Each of these—(a) and (b)—are identical in true value and worth $200,000 after taxes. Now, all Roth accumulations and distributions can generally be tax free. In effect, Fred has "switched" a $60,000 savings account into a savings instrument or investment within the Roth. (He'll gain from this transaction since the account's interest won't be taxed anymore.)

Realize, however, that while it is unlikely, it *is* possible that a Roth distribution can be taxed. Here are the rules. After the conversion is made, distributions come first from contributions, then from the converted sum, and finally from earnings during the next 5 years. If anything is taxed, it will be the earnings. There could also be a penalty tax pre-age 59½.

A 401(k) ROLLOVER INTO AN IRA

The other million dollar question is whether to actually roll over your 401(k) into an IRA at termination of employment, or retirement (or via an in-service, non-hardship withdrawal). The answer depends on your facts and circumstances.

On the one hand, you may not have a choice. If you're in a plan that forces out the funds, and you want to defer taxes, you'll definitely want to roll over the funds to defer the tax bill. Be sure to have the 401(k) trustee transfer the funds directly to a separate IRA, rather than to you. If not, the plan will withhold 20 percent in taxes on the distribution. Let's say you receive a gross distribution of $200,000 and the plan trustee withholds $40,000 in taxes. If you roll over, you'll need to find $40,000 to go with your check for $160,000 from that trustee, Otherwise, you'll actually owe additional taxes on the $40,000 withheld in taxes. (Once you find this tax money, however, there will be some good news; the $40,000 the IRS now has in withheld taxes will count against taxes you owe on other income. In other words, you won't have to come up with these taxes twice.)

Sounds bizarre, but it's true. Any money withheld is considered a "distribution eligible for rollover." And if you are under age 59½ you could pay a 10 percent penalty tax as well. That's why it's best to have the QP trustee transfer your $200,000 distribution *directly* to an IRA.

Here are other general guidelines that can help you determine whether to make the rollover.

The answer is probably "no" if:

- *Your 401(k) holds appreciated employer stock!* If you don't roll over, you'll pay mere capital gains on a sale. Or you roll over the stock and pay all taxes later. Here's an example: Let's say your 401(k) account purchased employer stock currently worth $200,000 for merely $40,000. You retire and take distribution of the shares. If you don't roll over, $40,000 is taxed as ordinary income now and any excess on a sale is capital gain. If these are rolled over, *all* distributions from the traditional IRA will be ordinary income. Normally, ordinary income is taxed at higher rates than capital gains.

  The bottom line: You'll have to choose between (a) $40,000 in ordinary income now and $160,000 (plus or minus) in personal capital gains later, or (b) $200,000 (plus or minus) in ordinary income later from IRA distributions.

- *You'll work for the employer past age 70½*—and don't need the money! Don't take the distribution. With a 401(k), you won't have to take any RMDs until actual retirement. With a traditional IRA, you would need to take RMDs.

- *Creditor protection is an issue!* Generally, qualified plans (QPs) give more shelter than IRAs, as long as money stays in the plan.

- You are comfortable with investment choices made in the account.

The answer is probably "yes" if:

- *You are considering marriage!* Roll over, probably. A new spouse has marital rights in a QP; there are no automatic marital rights in an IRA.

- *You want to control the QP money!* Roll over to an IRA. You'll have virtually any savings or investment option in a self-directed IRA. You might even roll over money in, say, a 401(k) account before you leave your employer. Let's say you are in your 40s or 50s and have a 401(k) account that has $25,000 in employer profit sharing/matching contributions. Yet the investments haven't done well. Or the administrative costs are high. Frankly, you'd rather take this $25,000 (and any earnings), roll it over to a self-directed IRA, and fully manage its savings/investment options. To do this, the 401(k) must have an "in-service, nonhardship withdrawal" option. If it does, you don't have to terminate employment or retire to obtain this money. Just follow the requirements spelled out in the plan's summary plan description or trust document. Further, if you are age 59½, you can withdraw and roll over all of your contributions (and earnings) as well.

To sum up, there are a number of factors to consider when exploring traditional IRAs versus Roth IRAs, and the merits of transferring money from an employer-sponsored 401(k) into an IRA. If you're uncertain, a financial planner is a must. I don't suggest reading up and doing this without help. Whichever IRA you choose, make sure to familiarize yourself with the all rules concerning distributions. The rules are seldom obvious; unfortunately, most account owners and beneficiaries learn the hard way. The books are full of these examples. Don't become one of them.

WHAT YOU NEED TO KNOW
IF YOU INHERIT AN IRA

The rules can depend on whether you are a spouse or nonspouse beneficiary.

If you are the spouse, ownership of the account passes to you. If you have a traditional IRA, this means you can convert it to a Roth IRA, if you choose. (Nonspouse beneficiaries cannot convert to a Roth.)

Second, if you are not the spouse, you are *not* permitted to roll over the account and put it in your name. It must be kept in the original owner's name, that is, "FBO (for benefit of) John Smith."

Third, as a nonspouse beneficiary, you will have to take a first distribution (RMD) by December 31st of the year following the account owner's death. The amount of that distribution will be based on your actual remaining life expectancy according to IRS Tables. (A spouse-beneficiary under age 70½ can normally keep the account intact until then, when RMDs will begin for him or her.)

Fourth, if a beneficiary doesn't need RMDs, he or she can disclaim the account in favor of a contingent beneficiary without making a taxable gift. Disclaimers are a complex subject that I won't cover here. Check with a lawyer and get the rules and tax consequences.

Fifth, any beneficiary may want to name a new beneficiary or transfer the account to a new IRA custodian or trustee. Look to the custodial agreement for alternatives. If you don't have the custodial agreement, search for the IRA provider on the Web and download its forms on-line.

To help you make any such decisions, meet with your financial advisor as soon as possible after you receive the inheritance. I'm serious about this; a delay here could be costly.

IRAS/QPS: A BRIEF ASSET PROTECTION ANALYSIS

If you want to protect your assets from claimants, IRAs—and QPs especially—are a great choice. They not only confer terrific tax advantages, but also significant asset protection in bankruptcy— and out. With IRAs, the level of protection varies from state to state, as I will explain next.

How ironic then that you don't have to be in a collections hassle, lawsuit, or bankruptcy to lose the money in an IRA. Nope. Access is so immediate that account owners or beneficiaries can easily do themselves in. If they're wastrels or poor money managers, they can blow the account on luxuries or "emergencies." Once that happens, it's probably too late to return money to the account and its tax- and creditor-protected status. For this reason, it's always better to borrow money before using up an IRA.

Beneficiaries can make huge mistakes, like retitling IRAs in the wrong name. They may think their inherited IRA is *theirs* and not even marital property in a divorce. However, courts tend to put everything "on the table" in marital situations; that IRA can disappear as quickly as the marriage itself. This is reality.

As a preventative measure, keep good records that trace where an inherited IRA came from. Arrange marital agreements that spell out which IRA belongs to each spouse. Although it may sound clichéd, "an ounce of prevention is worth a pound of cure."

That said, here are the some specifics on where IRAs/QPs may—and may not be—protected from creditors.

Protection for Account Owner and Plan Participant Funds in IRAs/QPs

Nonbankruptcy general creditors and lawsuits

Outside of bankruptcy, funds in most qualified plans (QPs) are fully shielded under federal law—the Employee Retirement Income Security Act of 1974 (ERISA). Funds in IRAs aren't protected by federal law. If there is shelter, it is under state laws only; normally, there is full protection, but these laws are tricky. (Sometimes there are waiting periods, limits on the protection, or other subtleties, so consult an attorney for help.) Here's a state law breakdown for IRAs in 2008. Be sure to check for any changes since then.

Forty-two states give full protection for traditional IRAs. These states are the exceptions: California, Georgia, Maine, Minnesota, Nebraska, North Dakota, and South Carolina, which safeguard the account essentially to the extent necessary for support of the debtor, spouse, and dependents. Wyoming offers no protection for traditional accounts.

Roths are fully protected from creditors in 36 states. California, Georgia, Maine, Minnesota, Nebraska, North Dakota (up to $200,000, *unless* necessary to support debtor, spouse, or dependents), and South Carolina safeguard a Roth "to the extent necessary for support of the debtor, spouse, and dependents." Alabama, Mississippi, Montana, Nevada, South Carolina, West Virginia, and Wyoming offer little or no protection for Roths.

In bankruptcy

On October 17, 2005, Congress enacted the Bankruptcy Abuse Prevention and Consumer Protection Act of 2005 (BAPA). While it made bankruptcy more difficult, BAPA significantly updated how IRAs, 401(k)s, and pensions are treated if you become insolvent. Here is an overview of this confusing legislation as it pertains to IRAs/QPs:

- *401(k)s and pensions*: Presently, all assets in QPs are *fully* exempt from most creditor claims in bankruptcy—with a few exceptions. Depending on the state laws where you live, your assets may still not be exempt if you owe money for alimony, maintenance, and child support, or are behind on your taxes.

- *Annual deductible contribution IRAs*: These are protected similarly, but to a $1 million limit (2004) or up to a $1.095 million limit (April 1, 2007), adjusted for inflation.

- *Rollover IRAs*: When your IRA funds come from QPs, they have the full exemption given QPs. But you should separate these IRA rollovers from annual contribution accounts. Keep a good paper trail; in the event of a future bankruptcy, this will show that a rollover IRA has full protection rather than being counted within the $1 million limit, adjusted for inflation.

Protection for IRA/QP Distributions to Account Owners and Plan Participants

In general

It's one thing to have funds in an IRA/QP that are protected from general creditors and in bankruptcy. It's another matter to shelter cash actually distributed from the fund or account.

QP/IRA distributions

In short, most funds *inside* QPs and IRAs are protected in bankruptcy under BAPA. With regard to nonbankruptcy general creditor situations, funds *inside* most QPs are sheltered under ERISA's federal law; funds *inside* IRAs are sheltered only under state laws.

When it comes to protection for distributions from IRAs and QPs, the law is less clear. Before BAPA, federal courts weren't too friendly to bankrupt debtors. Prison inmates may have suffered the most; there are at least three pre-BAPA cases where a creditor garnisheed QP pension incomes in an inmate's bank account. However, state courts have sometimes sheltered payments allocated to your support.

After BAPA, some think that IRA/QP distributions are protected from claimants. I'm not so sure. In 2005, an IRA owner pledged his $500,000 account to secure a loan. Then, when he was in bankruptcy proceedings, the court said the IRA was not protected since he had taken a "distribution" when the account was pledged.

The bottom line: It may be that distributions from IRAs/QPs are available to all creditors who can get there quickly and attach the funds. My suggestion: Don't give up. Have your lawyer carefully check your state laws regarding whether a creditor can attach account owner payments from an IRA/QP. He or she may find that QP pension or IRA money received for support of self and family is specifically safeguarded. If you live in a state where annuity incomes are protected under separate laws, acquire an IRA payout annuity (an IRA single premium immediate annuity). This annuity income, paid over your IRS life expectancy, will also qualify as RMDs. And always keep paper trails where bank deposits are traceable from an IRA/QP into another investment or resource.

Protection for Beneficiaries Who Inherit an IRA/QP

Once a spouse-beneficiary assumes control and rolls over the account, some think the new IRA should still be protected from creditors in bankruptcy. A nonspouse-beneficiary cannot roll the account to a personal IRA; therefore, his or her inherited IRA should probably not be shielded. (Indeed, a Texas court in 2007 considered this issue. A mother died, leaving an IRA to her bankrupt son. Since this was an "inherited" IRA, the court left the account unprotected; it reasoned that he had not put funds into the account and the law protected only the contributor.)

Regarding account distributions to beneficiaries, here are some suggestions: For extra layers of creditor protection, arrange to have payments come from annuities or IRA trusts that have spendthrift clauses. Pay distributions to trusts for beneficiaries instead of making payments directly to these persons. Finally, create paper trails to show when distributions were used for your support.

In conclusion, IRAs—traditional and Roth—offer terrific asset protection advantages. A financial advisor can help you determine which kind better suits your needs. Once you've set up the account, make sure you know—and play by—the rules so you can enjoy all of your money, rather than paying unnecessary penalties. And be sure to resist the urge to drain the fund yourself, if you're in a cash crunch.

Let's look next at the fourth and last cornerstone of a solid financial foundation—home ownership.

HOME OWNERSHIP: BASIC AND ADVANCED STRATEGIES

Somebody said to me, "But the Beatles were anti-materialistic." That's a huge myth. John and I literally used to sit down and say, "Now, let's write a swimming pool."
—*Paul McCartney*

Would it surprise you to learn that you can use your own home's appreciation as a wellspring for retirement income? You probably can. Don't look to a personal residence for direct cash flow. However, you may be able to tap the home's equity as a *source* of income in retirement.

I wish I could say this unequivocally. Not so long ago, I could. It was a given that one's home would *always* grow in value. That's no longer true—not after the real estate meltdown that started in 2007 and seemed to go on forever. So let me caution you to discuss my suggestions with a real estate or financial planning professional, and an accountant. Then take *their* advice—which will be tailored to your facts, circumstances, and market conditions at the time—rather than my suggestions, which are more general in nature. Also keep in mind my underlying message: *safety*. Remember that the government and the insurance carriers are the only ones who can guarantee safety. Finally, realize that I am citing a 5 percent growth rate in the examples below only for convenience, as I have done throughout the book.

That said, I still consider a personal residence a retirement income cornerstone, along with life insurance, annuities, and IRAs/QPs. Home ownership meets my standards for tax advantages and asset protection. In fact, one of the greatest blessings of home ownership is the homestead exemption, which can protect personal residence equity from the claims of most creditors. Of course, state exemptions vary greatly. Florida, Iowa, Kansas, South Dakota, and Texas currently exempt unlimited dollar value, but Delaware, Maryland, New Jersey, and Pennsylvania have no specific homestead exemption.

In addition, here are the two main tax advantages of owning your own home:

- A homeowner can deduct interest on a home mortgage loan (of up to $1 million). When you refinance, you can deduct interest on a loan up to $100,000.

- When a married couple sells their home, any profit up to $500,000 is tax free; for a single taxpayer, that drops to $250,000 in tax free profit. (Profit is any gain over the purchase price and cost of improvements.) In either case, to qualify for the tax exemption, the couple (or individual) must have lived in the home for at least two of the last 5 years immediately prior to the sale.

Yes, that's right—if you meet the requirements, investment in a personal residence can take you from tax-deductible cost (when you deduct interest on a home mortgage) to presumed gains (on the profits of the home) that are tax free. That sounds almost too good to be true. Fortunately, it isn't, if your home appreciates as anticipated. Given these assumptions, it's not much of a stretch to consider a home mortgage a tax-favored savings opportunity. If you are in your 40s or even younger, one simple strategy you can use to generate more income for your retirement years, is to "reach" a little and purchase a bit larger residence than you may need. Voila! If your home appreciates, sell it at a (tax free) profit, downsize to a less expensive home in retirement, and then sink your profits into annuities or cash value life insurance, using the income-boosting strategies I've written about earlier.

A PERSONAL RESIDENCE AS A SOURCE OF RETIREMENT INCOME

To illustrate the kinds of gains that may be possible with a home, let's start with the following example. Let's say you are married and looking to acquire a home. It is in foreclosure, priced at $250,000, but probably worth more like $400,000. You've found a lender who will charge 6 percent interest on a 20-year, 100 percent loan. (This is not out of the question—the lender could be a family member who believes the home's value is considerably more than its current price.) In fact, a real estate appraisal indicates that you are making a good buy.

Since you see good growth potential here, you'd like to use the property eventually for a retirement income, if that's possible. How do you analyze this opportunity for all that it is worth? Well, let's make a few assumptions and find out.

THE TAX ECONOMICS OF HOME OWNERSHIP

Let's assume you are in a 30 percent tax bracket. First, try itemizing tax deductions (including mortgage interest), which helps if the deductions exceed the standard deduction—$11,400 jointly in 2010. There are a few more things to know about this deduction, but nothing that should affect you.

At 6 percent loan interest, your annual mortgage payment on a 20-year, $250,000 fixed loan is $21,800—$436,000 in total input. The deduction works this way. That 1st year, your write-off is about $15,000 (6 percent × $250,000); in year 20, you'll claim virtually zero. Over 20 years, your average allocation to principal is $12,500 ($250,000 ÷ 20). The average interest is $9,300 (1/20 × $186,000 [$436,000 less $250,000]). Therefore, your average annual tax savings will be $2,790 (30 percent × $9,300 in deductions).

Here's a more accurate way to look at tax savings on an average annual interest payment of $9,300.

Let's say your other itemized deductions (medical, charitable, etc.) are $7,000. Since you could claim a standard deduction of $11,400 anyway, $4,400 ($11,400 less $7,000) of the average interest payment of $9,300 is a wasted deduction.

Therefore, only $4,900 ($9,300 less $4,400) is a useful deduction. A deduction for $4,900 in a 30 percent bracket really saves $1,470 in taxes (30 percent × $4,900). It reduces actual cash outlay to $20,330 ($21,800 less $1,470 in tax savings) each year, on average.

—

Now, let's look some 20 years out. Let's assume your net loan payment remains constant at $20,330 a year and your home appreciates at a steady 5 percent rate from $250,000 to $650,000. You are able to sell the home and pocket $650,000 ($20,330 × 31.97).

Good news! Your profit of $400,000 ($650,000 less $250,000) is tax free. To get even more precise and pinpoint the actual rate of return on your initial $250,000 investment, use this equation: $650,000 ÷ $20,330. Since the quotient is 31.97, your net return is a steady 4.75 percent compounded annually over these 20 years. (In other words, $1 saved annually over 20 years will build to $31.97, if it earns a steady 4.75 percent annual rate of return. Since $650,000 ÷ $20,330 is 31.97, your home's investment has also earned 4.75 percent.)

No doubt, closing costs at point of sale reduce your net profit. For example, if closing costs were $25,000, the net is only $625,000, leaving a $375,000 profit. That reduces the quotient to 30.74 ($625,000 ÷ $20,330). The tax free rate of return declines from 4.75 percent to 4.25 percent, compounded annually over a 20-year period.

You can get even better results if you take out an "interest only" (or almost "interest only") loan where you don't amortize principal. You only pay interest. If you could get, say, a $250,000, 6 percent interest-only loan, it might work like this.

Your annual deductible interest payment is $15,000. Since $4,400 of this is wasted (as I explained previously), the useful net deductible interest is $10,600 ($15,000 less $4,400). It saves $3,180 (30 percent × $10,600) in taxes, which reduces your net annual interest cost to $11,820 ($15,000 less $3,180). After 20 years, when you sell the home for $650,000, you repay the $250,000 loan, and pocket $400,000. The quotient is 33.84 ($400,000 ÷ $11,820). This increases your annual compounded rate of return to about 5.25 percent.

In short, it's best taxwise to pay mostly interest and very little in principal because you can never get a deduction for loan principal payments themselves—that is, assuming your home does appreciate, say at 5 percent per annum in my example.

In the illustration I gave earlier, the gain was only $400,000, which is $100,000 below the tax free limit. Of course, if the gain gets to $500,000 or more, any home improvements you've made and documented could help you get greater tax mileage here. Let's say the sale price is $800,000. After 20 years when a $250,000 loan is repaid, the gross profit is $550,000, with only $500,000 tax free. If good records show $50,000 in improvements, your profit becomes $500,000, and everything escapes income taxes.

If you are of a mind to buy and sell your home for the purpose of gaining a tax free profit, you can theoretically do this every 2 years. In other words, you can complete a tax free sale on your next home after a 2-year waiting period—then repeat this strategy again and again. In each case, however, your deduction could not exceed interest on a $1 million home loan, and your tax free gain on each sale cannot exceed $500,000 for married couples filing jointly, or $250,000 for a single taxpayer.

That's a bit much for most people, however. Fortunately, there is a way to access home equity without actually selling the house. Let's look more closely at something called a *home equity line of credit* (HELOC).

HELOCS as a Source of Home Equity

Let's say your home has a considerable amount of built-in profit, and you obtain a $100,000 HELOC at 6 percent interest. (I am choosing $100,000 here because HELOCs up to $100,000 give the opportunity to claim an itemized tax deduction for interest paid.) The lender will secure this loan with your home. Typically, you pay interest only. You may invest the loan proceeds or use this money for any reason at any time. Here are some possibilities. Take loan proceeds and:

- Buy a car and pay off credit card bills. You can deduct the HELOC's interest.

- Invest in, say, 8 percent second mortgages. The 8 percent investment interest is taxable; the HELOC's interest is deductible.

- Invest in the stock market. Any gains are taxable; your HELOC's interest is deductible.

- Acquire a single premium deferred annuity (SPDA). Your deferred profit is taxable eventually; unfortunately, your HELOC's interest is specifically *not* deductible. Simply put, tax law doesn't allow an interest deduction if the loan proceeds are redeployed in a tax-deferred or tax free savings vehicle. *Since there is no advantage here, I don't suggest this!*

- Invest in tax free municipal bonds. Your bond interest may be tax free; your HELOC interest, again, is specifically *not* deductible. *Don't do this either!*

- Acquire a single premium life insurance contract for $100,000. Since the contract is likely a "MEC" (Modified Endowment Contract), any withdrawals of profit are taxable; again, your HELOC loan interest is specifically *not* deductible. *Don't do this either!*

Beware of an often-touted—although ultimately unworkable—strategy in which HELOC loan proceeds are reemployed immediately in a life insurance contract in which loan interest is presumably tax deductible; then, policy loans are taken tax free! That program, as it is usually packaged, doesn't work! *In fact, it will likely cause (a) nondeductible HELOC interest and (b) taxable loans from the life insurance contract.* That's not a good result.

Remember, if you obtain a $100,000 HELOC, *don't* assume that the loan's interest is always tax deductible. Realize that this can change based on the nature of any investments or savings vehicles that you obtain with the proceeds. Also realize that tax laws that pertain to interest deductions and investment income are complicated and can change. Finally, I assume that you'll still have considerable equity (after the HELOC) in your home.

The bottom line: To engage in a HELOC/retirement income plan, always have your advisors develop the right strategy based on your individual circumstances.

Reverse Mortgages for an Income in Retirement

This strategy—used to tap home equity in retirement—has also received a considerable amount of press. Unlike the misguided HELOC/life insurance strategy I just mentioned, however, this one *is* worth considering.

According to the U.S. Census Bureau, 50 percent of homeowners over age 65 own their homes free and clear of any debt or mortgage. (Some 80.5 percent of individuals age 65 or older own their homes.) Equity in a home might be the greatest source of net worth for a substantial number of these retirees. Given that and current economic conditions, a *reverse mortgage* (RM)—if you are age 62 or older—can be a useful strategy to generate more income in retirement.

When you take out a RM, you actually receive a portion of the home's equity tax free. (To me, tax free makes perfect sense. If you sold the house instead, the profit—$250,000 or $500,000—would presumably be tax free as well.) However the process involves complex calculations and is somewhat daunting. To make things easier, I recommend reading *Reverse Mortgages for Dummies* by Sarah Glendon Lyons and John E. Lucas (Wiley Publishing, 2005). This quick read should answer all your questions about RMs.

Most RMs are insured by the Federal Housing Authority (FHA). Before applying, seniors are required to undergo loan counseling. The counselor must be approved by the U.S. Department of Housing and Urban Development (HUD)—which is the government's way of making sure the loan applicant receives unbiased and complete borrower information. (To contact HUD for an approved counselor, call 1-800-569-4287.) Non-FHA-insured reverse mortgages may involve higher risk and cost to homeowners, so use extra caution when considering those.

If you are approved for a RM, the amount you can borrow will depend on market value, your age, and current interest rates. You still own and live in the home. You'll repay the loan (with interest) when you move out, sell, or die. The funds for repayment will come from the equity in your home. If there is remaining equity, it belongs to you or your heirs; if the loan balance exceeds market value, you won't owe anything.

RM lenders make nonrecourse loans. This assures you that when the home is sold, sales proceeds are considered payment in full even if the loan balance at the time of sale is greater than what is received from the buyer. Consequently, the lender will be conservative in calculating a loan advance. In other words, the interest rate may be a little higher and the assumed rate of home appreciation a little lower.

Let's say you choose a Home Equity Conversion Mortgage (HECM) offered by HUD. Here, you'll pay a Mortgage Insurance Premium (MIP); this protects against a loan balance that exceeds the home's sale price.

A Sample Reverse Mortgage Calculation

Estimated Home Value	$500,000
Loan Availability (a)	$225,000
Total Fees and Costs (b)	$15,000
Debt Payoff Advance I	0
Net Cash for You	$210,000
Expected Interest Rate (e)	6%

(a) The older the borrower, the higher the loan available.
(b) Estimated closing costs, fees, and loan servicing charges. I am assuming the home is debt free; if not, all loans must be paid off to obtain the RM.

(e) The anticipated loan interest rate.

The bottom line: In this case, the RM lender is aware of initial and annual costs, fees, and charges "folded" into the RM loan. It has calculated the loan plus interest that is accumulating over the years. Finally, it anticipates that these obligations will be covered by the home's value, which will appreciate at say 3 to 4 percent annually. Consequently, with MIP insurance covering any shortfall, the lender is willing to loan the "Net Cash Available" with no payments of principal or interest *ever*. At your death (or sale of the house), there will be a payoff with any remaining cash distributed to your heirs (or you, if you are still alive when the house sells). Realize that as the borrower, you must pay annual real estate taxes and remain in the home. You can use the RM proceeds for *anything*; life insurance, long-term care coverage, and annuities should probably be on the list.

An Intrafamily Sale of a Personal Residence

If RMs don't appeal to you, consider this alternative. You are married, and you may have an heir, typically a son or daughter, willing and financially able to buy your home and pay monthly mortgage payments and home expenses. Then, your family member can lease the premises back to you. There are a number of possibilities, and again, each involves complex calculations. Briefly, here are two examples:

1. Your $500,000 home is debt free with a paid-off mortgage. You sell the home to an adult son, who finances the purchase. Then, you use the cash to purchase a single premium income annuity that pays, say, $40,000 annually for 20 years or so. Finally, you pay rent to your son. If it doesn't cover

your son's mortgage, he must be able to absorb any shortfall on his loan payment.

2. You sell this home to your son in exchange for a lifetime income from him. Then, you lease the premises from your son. Your lease payment helps finance his payment to you. Of course, you can agree to any number of factors in calculating who pays how much. These arrangements will have estate, gift, and income tax implications, so you'll need to involve your lawyer in the planning process. He or she will advise you on tax factors and prepare any legal agreements between your son and you. You'll also need an accountant or someone to crunch numbers that involve you and your son's tax brackets and financial circumstances. Because there are a number of complexities involved, I won't confuse you with an example.

The bottom line: If you have children or other close family members in sound financial circumstances, an intrafamily sale and lease back can be tailored in a number of interesting ways. Even if you can work out the calculations, please use a trusted accountant, lawyer, and financial planner to fine-tune numbers. (I can almost guarantee that an advisor's conference will be worthwhile.) Your advisors can be of tremendous help here, especially when it comes to tax and estate factors—just as they would be if you were pursuing a reverse mortgage.

PERSONAL RESIDENCES: A BRIEF ASSET PROTECTION ANALYSIS

All 50 states have "homestead" exemptions that protect personal residences from creditors and bankruptcy seizures. Homestead exemptions refer to equity in a primary residence and are meant to prevent forced sales of homes to meet demands of creditors. The shelter normally is automatic; however, a homeowner must sometimes file for protection. Forced sales that simply satisfy mortgages, mechanics liens, or property taxes are not exempt.

In most states, homestead exemptions are low ($5,000 to $100,000), but they are rising. However, Arkansas, District of Columbia, Florida, Iowa, Kansas, Massachusetts, Minnesota, Nevada, Oklahoma, Rhode Island, South Dakota, and Texas have high limits (or virtually no limits). Florida's liberal law may even protect sales proceeds put in a bank account as long as the homeowner has a genuine intent to purchase another home in Florida.

Be aware, however, that the Bankruptcy Abuse Prevention and Consumer Protection Act of 2005 (BAPA) may limit a state's "unlimited" homestead exemption in bankruptcy to $125,000. The law works this way.

If a state gives greater than a $125,000 homestead exemption, the homeowner must own the residence for 1,215 days (over 3 years) before filing for bankruptcy. Otherwise only $125,000 of equity is sheltered.

As expected, there are exceptions to the $125,000 cap. In one amazing case, a Florida couple on the eve of bankruptcy moved from a modest residence to an expensive $4.5 million home that they had owned for more than 1,215 days (but had not previously resided in) before their bankruptcy filing. Lucky for them! The court gave unlimited protection following Florida law.

To sum up—homestead laws protect at least some of your home's equity from creditors. Since such safeguards exist, don't begrudge the mortgage payments that build this equity. You may want it some day as a source for income in retirement.

The bottom line: Home ownership can be advantageous for anyone looking for another source of income in retirement. As I have shown, one possibility is to sell and pocket any profit tax free, then downsize into a smaller home, and redeploy your gain into life insurance and annuities. Another is an interest-only home equity line of credit. (If you can save or invest and achieve returns that exceed the deductible loan interest cost, this could work.) You can also take a reverse mortgage to gain extra income. Or you can work out an intrafamily sale as I've described. Speak with your financial advisor to determine if any of these options—or similar strategies— best suit your individual circumstances.

SOMETHING FOR BENEFICIARIES TOO

Money isn't everything but it sure keeps you in
touch with your children.
—*J. Paul Getty*

Discussions about retirement income planning often lead to decisions about what to leave for loved ones—and how best to do it. A lot of this is personal choice. Some feel fine about "spending their children's inheritance"—although that's not as easy to do as it sounds. Others are happier placing family (and/or friends) and charities ahead of themselves. In fact, most individuals who buy income annuities reject slightly larger life-only payouts in favor of lower payouts with refunds or installments that provide something for beneficiaries as well.

I can't help you make those decisions. But I can explain the smartest, most efficient ways to pass along what you have worked so hard to acquire. And if you are one of those people afraid there won't be anything left, your fears are probably groundless. Frankly, if you do your retirement income planning correctly, it's *difficult* to die broke. I've seen IRA owners limit their withdrawals to required minimum distributions (RMDs), because they worry incessantly about having claimants come after their money, paying taxes unnecessarily, and/or someday running out of money. In truth, they end up with larger accounts when they die than they had at age 70½.

Financial planners can help you think through all the possibilities here. (They typically combine retirement income planning with life insurance coverage, so retirees and beneficiaries both win.)

As you begin thinking about these matters, you'll want to keep a clear head about what is passing to whom, through what vehicle. In other words, as your personal assets—those titled in your name—tend to shift from customary or conventional ones (such as CDs, treasuries, mutual funds, stocks, etc.) into unconventional retirement-oriented structures (cash value life insurance, annuities, and IRAs/QPs), the route by which they pass to your heirs after your death changes too. In short, conventional assets pass through a will. But the unconventional assets I named are distributed under forms by beneficiary designations. Consequently, beneficiary designation forms will assume an important role in your overall planning.

For that reason, I suggest that you assemble your beneficiary forms and discuss primary, contingent, and successor designations with your estate and retirement income team. Ask them about insurance/annuity settlement option income plans too. (Be sure to learn about trusts as beneficiaries for any remaining retirement assets.)

Everything should be coordinated, keeping optimal tax and asset protection planning strategies in mind. This will help make sure that your loved ones will enjoy what's left at your death the same way that these assets benefitted you. After all, that is the point, isn't it?

Now let's move ahead to the nitty-gritty. I will explain the keys to good planning for your beneficiaries. They'll like this discussion. After all, it's infinitely more fun to inherit than bequeath, as they say. Let's have a conversation in a structured question and answer format—as if you were at an estate planning seminar. Over the course of the "seminar," we'll cover:

- wills and trusts compared with beneficiary designations
- choices in beneficiary forms
- settlement options that pay incomes to beneficiaries
- beneficiary tax deductions for transfer taxes paid by the estate
- a beneficiary controlled trust
- annuity incomes moving into a life insurance policy
- an inherited "stretch" annuity
- a spouse as annuity beneficiary
- a pre-October 21, 1979, variable annuity
- IRAs in second marriages
- a beneficiary's 401(k) roll over to an IRA
- a spouse as IRA roll over beneficiary
- a "stretch" IRA for family
- leaving an IRA to a trust
- a "Who is your IRA beneficiary?" discussion

Ready to begin? You'll ask the questions, and I'll give the answers.

WILLS AND TRUSTS COMPARED WITH BENEFICIARY DESIGNATIONS

Q. I am married with two children and have wills and a trust for them. I'm concerned about beneficiary designations. What controls the outcome—wills and trusts or a beneficiary form?

Answer: This question comes up frequently. Once more, it depends on whether you have mostly conventional (traditional) or unconventional assets. Again, the former pass under wills and trusts; the latter by beneficiary forms.

The problem is that lawyers write wills, trusts, and deeds; salespersons and people untrained in the law normally handle beneficiary designations. Too often, a beneficiary arrangement is done in haste and a poor decision made without considering the lasting effects.

I am not saying that you always need a lawyer or financial planner when you complete beneficiary forms. However, you should be aware of all of your choices and take enough time with these forms to get things straight.

Q. I'm still confused. Let's assume that I have $500,000 in a personally owned treasury bond. As a conventional asset, you say that this could pass under my will. What happens if I don't have a will? Or a trust?

Answer: Let me explain most of the possibilities.

Your conventional assets

- If you don't have a will or trust, your treasury bond will pass "intestate"—meaning there is no valid will. Under laws where you live, your spouse will likely receive one-half of the total estate's value; your children could divide the remainder. You might say that they "inherit under the state's will." If you have a valid personal will instead, your treasury will pass "testate." By the laws of most states, your spouse must still receive at least one-half of the total estate's value; the remainder will pass as specified in the document. Everything is distributed directly to family—or possibly a trust for their benefit.

- Whether passing intestate or testate, conventional assets will be part of a probate "estate." The estate is monitored (and protected) by a probate court. There are costs for administrative matters and fees for a lawyer's advice. Assets will be available to estate creditors and those to whom you owe money when you die. It is possible for beneficiaries, heirs, and others to contest wills and claim fraud or undue influence when you signed the document.

- When testate assets pass to a trust (and not directly to individuals), there potentially are a number of advantages. This "testamentary" trust can provide management, flexibility, enhanced creditor protection, and tax planning alternatives. As some say, trusts can even allow a testator (the person whose will it is) to "control things from the grave." These advantages need to be weighed against negatives such as trustee fees, and trust accounting and tax preparation costs.

- There is an alternative to a testamentary trust. It is called a revocable living trust. Here, someone establishes a trust while alive and typically transfers conventional assets to the trust, which becomes a "will substitute" eventually; in other words, its assets are maintained or distributed to family as specified in the trust agreement (instead of under a will).

- Consequently, "living trusts" can sidestep a more expensive probate process. Some say it's not likely that a living trust will be contested. It will also give you and your family a preliminary look at what happens when deaths occur or circumstances change. Of course, you can always modify or cancel your revocable living trust.

Observation: Trusts are an integral part of the U.S. legal and financial system. When it comes to flexibility, creditor protection, and tax planning, our laws definitely favor trust arrangements *for* someone over outright gifts and bequests *to* that person.

Q. I also have a $500,000 life insurance policy. Since it is an unconventional asset, what should be done on the beneficiary form?

Answer: This can get tricky. Basically, life insurance, annuities, and IRAs and 401(k) funds that pass under beneficiary forms go directly to family or charity, or a trust for their benefit (typically a revocable living trust).

It's also possible to keep life insurance and annuity money with the insurer under "settlement options" that pay out incomes (instead of lump sums) to individuals or trusts.

Let's look at what happens in general, with beneficiaries listed on beneficiary designation forms. Then, we'll consider settlement options that handle money left with insurance carriers.

Choices in beneficiary forms

There can be a number of innocent and unintended consequences on typical beneficiary designation forms. For instance:

- If a payee is, say, "my wife, Mary" (or "my spouse, Mary"), and you are divorced from Mary, it's possible that she will still receive the money. *Be aware*: State laws typically "revoke" bequests of conventional assets to a previous spouse. But, when unconventional assets pass by beneficiary forms, language on the form may control the outcome. Therefore, it's important that divorce documents cover what happens and that beneficiary forms reflect what spouses agreed to in the divorce papers.

- An individual beneficiary might predecease his or her benefactor with no contingent beneficiary listed on the form.

Then, the money passes to someone's estate and possibly to creditors or strangers.

- An individual beneficiary could be disabled, incapacitated, in divorce, or a minor where there is no protection from the system. Here a trust-beneficiary could be the solution. The reason is that trust language can be crafted to solve most every circumstance that comes up.

- Let's say you list "my children, equally" as direct beneficiaries. Your daughter predeceases her brother and he receives everything at your death. If she has family, they'll get nothing. Would you want that?

- The results are much different if a beneficiary is, say, "lawful issue *per stirpes*." Here, if your daughter dies before you, her children "step up" and receive her one-half share. Your son still receives his one-half share. (That seems reasonable, even though her spouse would get nothing.) If they are minors, a trust fund for them would be better; otherwise, a court might have to supervise a guardian of the minor's property.

- If beneficiaries (of annuities and insurance) are members of a group, some may want cash while others could prefer settlement option incomes. A better approach may be separate policies payable to each person.

Settlement options that pay incomes to beneficiaries

When it comes to insurance and annuity settlement option incomes for beneficiaries, payments can be (a) *fixed amounts* (say $1,000 per month for as long as the money lasts); (b) amortized over a *fixed period* (10, 15, or 20 years); (c) *interest only,* where interest is paid and principal can be withdrawn in cash; (d) *lifetime* (where income is based on life expectancies of one or two beneficiaries); or (e) *life income with a period certain* (lifetime payments with a minimum term assured). Of course, an income under (a), (b), (d), or (e) will always include a combination of principal and interest amortized over the years involved.

Here are some observations about using settlement options for your insurance or annuity beneficiaries:

- Traditionally, most insurance death benefits have been lump sums paid to individuals—or trusts to benefit individuals. In fact, if you call an insurer's claims department and request beneficiary settlement income forms, the claims person on the phone may not know how to help you.

- If you want your beneficiary to have an income, make the settlement arrangement now. Otherwise, odds are that he or she will take the cash instead. (In fact, some insurers will "buckle" if an income beneficiary shows up with a lawyer and demands a lump sum instead. Ask your carrier what they'll do in this circumstance.)

- By arranging a beneficiary's income now, you'll be assuring him or her a management-free, safe, and steady cash flow that comes "every time, all the time, and anywhere in the world." If it is a lifetime income, it can't be outlived either. In my experience, beneficiaries like lump sums, but they *love* a regular income.

- Most states permit an income plan to have a "spendthrift" clause that protects payments from garnishment or attachment if your beneficiary gets a divorce or into financial trouble. (The important thing is whether state law safeguards the income after it is received by your beneficiary.) Generally, these laws give better protection when you make this arrangement yourself, rather than if it is made after your death.

- Settlement options do have negatives. For instance, the income is fixed and can be weakened by inflation. Interest rates on the unpaid balance tend to be low, say 2 to 4 percent. When a beneficiary dies, money left over from fixed amounts or fixed periods can belong to creditors in someone's estate. (That's why I always recommend naming *successor* beneficiaries, who receive any remaining payments. Otherwise, what's left will go to the first beneficiary's *estate*.) Finally, the amounts are usually set with no right to cash in for emergencies or other reasons.

- If you make the settlement option arrangement now, keep a right to change things up until your death. Otherwise, an irrevocable plan could keep you from policy loans or cash withdrawals for income in retirement. The reason is that carriers will opt to protect the beneficiary and refuse your requests for the money.

Observations: I believe settlement options that assure lifetime incomes will become more popular. You and your beneficiaries will select from true fixed, indexed, and variable payments. There will also be rights to commute or accelerate payments and more flexibility and liquidity for beneficiaries. In short, everything will become more user-friendly. That is a good thing.

To sum up, it's difficult to weigh all the possibilities for your loved ones. The important thing is that there are major differences with wills/trusts and beneficiary designations. Your retirement income team should coordinate everything into one smoothly working plan. Then, as your assets shift into unconventional assets—annuities, life policies, and IRAs/QPs—there won't be any painful slipups.

WHY AREN'T SETTLEMENT OPTIONS MORE POPULAR?

Settlement option payouts should be more popular, given their benefits. Why aren't they? I think there are several reasons.

First, most beneficiaries feel a "wealth affect" when they receive a large sum at one time. In other words, putting $100,000 on a financial statement seems better than receiving, say, a $600 monthly income for 20 years. Second, insurers don't promote settlement option incomes; for some reason they'd rather pay out cash and pay again to reacquire the money into a new life or annuity contract. Finally, insurance agents usually aren't paid to arrange death benefits under an income program.

Education is key. At some point, we will learn that capital is just as good as the income it provides. When this happens, settlement option payouts will become more popular.

BENEFICIARY TAX DEDUCTIONS FOR TRANSFER TAXES PAID BY THE ESTATE

Q. I have large holdings where there will surely be estate taxes. When my family inherits, could there be an income tax deduction for these taxes?

Answer: That's a very intelligent question. The answer is "Normally not!" The reason is that most inherited assets are tax paid where there is no income that can be offset with a deduction. It's the opposite when an annuity income or traditional IRA is inherited; here, there is a tax savings opportunity that's easy to overlook. (Technically, a deduction for estate taxes is claimed against income-in-respect-of-a-decedent—"hidden" income in an inherited asset that is waiting to be taxed.)

Example (1): Your children inherit a $200,000 traditional IRA where cashouts or RMDs are fully taxed as ordinary income. This account also incurs an $80,000 federal estate transfer tax that will be deductible on taxable IRA distributions. (So, the first $80,000 they withdraw will be tax free!)

Example (2): You own a $200,000 annuity payable to your son; it has $100,000 in tax-deferred growth that incurs a $40,000 federal estate transfer tax. The $40,000 estate tax is fully deductible as he pays income taxes on this profit.

In these examples, the deduction is allowable because an inherited asset includes income-in-respect-of-a-decedent.

It's easy to miss a deduction for estate taxes. Know that your estate could even pay its estate taxes from assets passing to your daughter or another person. But, since your son receives the IRA or annuity, he claims the deduction on its built-in income. Everyone needs to know the rules.

A BENEFICIARY-CONTROLLED TRUST

Q. Our family is really worried about what might come to pass in the near future. We want to protect everything as much as possible from the system. Is there something called a "beneficiary-controlled trust" that could help?

Answer: I am glad you asked this question. "Beneficiary-controlled trusts" can be an excellent planning choice. They give needed protection for conventional assets and added shelter to unconventional assets. Here's how these could work:

1. You create two trusts now (or in your will)—one for each of your children. On beneficiary forms, you name these trusts as beneficiaries of your unconventional assets. By will, you

bequeath any conventional assets to these trusts. Here's what your trusts might provide for each child:

- as trustee, both children will control all their money;
- as lifetime beneficiary, both children will be entitled to an income, trustee's fees and additional payments of principal as arranged;
- as trustee, each child can pay income to his or her children and let them pay the income taxes;
- a friend can be a "special trustee," to handle things if your children have an emergency or can't fend for themselves;
- your children could actually "rewrite" their trust to spell out who gets what at their deaths (and how their families ultimately receive everything).

2. Think of it! *You* establish these trusts, but your children virtually have complete control over their trust share, with asset protection possible for life. Under present tax law, there are other advantages. The trusts will own everything; as taxpayers, they pay taxes on income that your children don't take out. When the children die, the trusts spell out who inherits, but your children won't personally be making a gift or transfer then that incurs an estate tax.

In bridge tournaments, I occasionally play against Bill Gates, a bridge enthusiast like me. Whenever I see this interesting and benevolent man, I think about how his parents could have created a trust for him to initially acquire Microsoft stock. Then, as trustee, he would control everything but have all the creditor protection and tax advantages that our system allows. If you have in mind the next Microsoft or Berkshire-Hathaway, by all means ask a relative or friend to create a beneficiary controlled trust for you and have it own the business.

ANNUITIES

Annuity incomes moving into a life policy

Q. I am 65, healthy, and have a $400,000 single premium deferred annuity (SPDA) that cost only $50,000 in the 1980s. I have named my sister as the beneficiary. I am concerned because she'll pay over $100,000 in taxes on its profit, which is presently $350,000. Is there anything she or I can do to change that?

Answer: There is, but you have to make a "switch" now into life insurance. If you annuitize your present policy over, say, 20 years, you'll receive about $32,000 annually with only $2,500 (1/20 × $50,000) tax free each year. If you pay $8,850 in taxes at 30 percent on $29,500, your net cash will be $23,150 ($32,000 less $8,850). That should pay annual premiums on nearly $1 million in tax free life insurance.

The bottom line: Presently, you have a $400,000 annuity that is worth about $300,000 after taxes to your sister. A life policy more than triples this to $1 million tax free. If you intend the SPDA for an inheritance (and don't need your money now), annuitize into the life policy instead.

An inherited "stretch" annuity

Q. I own an SPDA that my son will want to annuitize when I die. Does he have another option that slows down the taxes?

Answer: He may! In 2001, one insurance company obtained a private IRS ruling that permitted "life expectancy" payouts for a beneficiary.

Example: Harold dies with a $200,000 annuity policy payable to Mary, age 65. She could cash out or receive level lifetime annuity income or a 20-year payout of, say, $16,000 annually. Under the ruling, she could take merely 1/20 or $10,000 in year 1; in year 2, she takes 1/19 of the account balance, 1/18 in year 3, and so on. This is a so-called stretch annuity with *increasing* (instead of level) payments—meaning lower income taxes now and more later.

Observation: This IRS ruling is private to the insurer and not available universally. You'll need to ask whether this stretch program (in lieu of annuitizing) is available for your policy. If it's workable, know that your son's payments and withdrawals will probably be taxed LIFO—*any taxable income first* (*and second, tax free principal*) until all profit in the policy is received. (LIFO is an acronym for "last-in, first-out.") If the withdrawals were taxed FIFO, they would be tax-free principal first—and second, taxable interest.

A spouse as annuity beneficiary

Q. I have an SPDA worth $500,000. It cost $100,000. My wife is the beneficiary. When I die, what should she know?

Example (1): John dies owning the policy, and the contract "matures" when he dies. Then, Mary, his spouse-beneficiary, can assume control of the policy. Now, she can defer taxable distributions until the actual maturity date, her death, or when she withdraws money from the policy.

Example (2): John dies as annuitant; his wife, Mary owns the policy. The contract "matures" and a lump sum becomes payable at his death. Here, Mary already owns the policy and cannot *assume* control. Consequently, she'll have merely 60 days to annuitize or pay taxes on a lump sum.

Note the differences in these annuity contracts. In example (1), Mary can assume control and defer taxes; in example (2), she will be subject to the 60-day rule. Everything depends on policy language and how the application was originally completed.

A pre-October 21, 1979, variable annuity

Q. I have annuities that date to the 1970s. One is a variable annuity (VA). Something tells me to pay close attention to this policy. Is my hunch correct?

Answer: Yes! Normally, all profit in inherited deferred annuities is taxable to a beneficiary. However, there is a major exception for VAs purchased before October 21, 1979. Here, the beneficiary's gain or profit will be tax free.

Example: You own a pre-October 21, 1979, VA that you acquired in the 1970s. It cost $50,000 but is worth a whopping $700,000. When your beneficiaries receive this money, they'll escape income taxes on profit to your date of death. If you cash in or exchange this annuity for a new policy, you'll lose this tax advantage.

Be aware: Pre-October 21, 1979, VAs are dwindling in number. Still it is very important that such VAs remain intact until the policyowner dies. It is a disaster to exchange them for another policy or withdraw the money before death! (That's because the first approach causes taxes on all profit remaining at death; the second taxes a withdrawal that would be tax free at death.) If you take either of these options, you will incur tax on money that could be tax free. If you keep the policy intact instead, all profit is tax free for your family or friends.

IRAs

IRAs in second marriages

Q. My second marriage is a good one. Still, I might want to name my sister beneficiary of a $300,000 IRA. How can I do this and provide for my wife as well?

Answer: Financial planners see this question often. Here are some thoughts: Obviously, you can leave other assets to your spouse.

However, you may have an agreement that she is to receive the IRA too. You can change this agreement if you both agree.

You could purchase life insurance (or a reversionary annuity) for her, to "cover" the agreement. Then, you could name your sister beneficiary of the IRA. (Alternately, the insurance could be for your sister with the IRA account for your spouse.) Again, you might need to adjust any marital agreements to cover changes in the planning.

A beneficiary's 401(k) rollover to an IRA

Q. When my children inherit my traditional IRA, they can take RMDs and "stretch out" taxable distributions over their lifetimes. If they inherit my 401(k) account, can they roll this money over to my IRA and take only RMDs from it as well?

Answer: You'd think so, but the law is quirky. When someone inherits a 401(k) account, the trustee can pay them RMDs directly from the plan. More likely, the trustee will force-out the money to beneficiaries and gain relief from on going management duties. Under present law, they'll have to cash out and pay ordinary income taxes at once. That's because only spouse-beneficiaries can receive distributions, assume control, and roll 401(k) funds to a personal IRA.

There are two ways around this problem. If the QP transfers your money *directly* to an IRA—a "direct rollover"—your children can take out merely RMDs. Arrange for the trustee to make the direct transfer or rollover; do *not* have the money come to your children or they will owe taxes on it. Alternately, the plan trustees might give your beneficiaries a "nontransferable" annuity where they can either annuitize or take RMDs.

The bottom line: Their IRA (or annuity) must be titled, "Joe Jones (you)—FBO, John Jones (your beneficiary)." FBO is short for "for the benefit of." If the transfer creates a Roth, your children also need to be eligible to make a Roth conversion, as I explain in chapter 8.

Finally, know you can sidestep all the complications that I've mentioned by taking your 401(k) money and making an IRA roll over before you die. Then, your beneficiaries will be able to take mere RMDs and avoid paying taxes all at once.

A spouse as IRA rollover beneficiary

Q. Let's say my wife names me beneficiary of her IRA. What happens to the account?

Answer: If you have total control and put your name on the account, it's as if it always has been yours. You can name a new beneficiary and take RMDs at age 70½, just like the original owner.

There is one matter your wife shouldn't overlook. You'll have full control, which means you can choose your new spouse, a friend, or children from a previous marriage as *your* beneficiary. If this concerns her, she should name a "spousal trust" beneficiary for you, which means that anything that remains after your death will go to successor beneficiaries named in the trust.

Be aware: When a spousal trust is beneficiary of an IRA, a spouse won't become owner of the account. Consequently, the law forces out more taxable money each year. There are computer programs that compare what happens when an account owner leaves an IRA to a spouse or a spousal trust. Essentially, the first option offers income tax advantages; the second allows more control over who gets the account someday.

A "stretch" IRA for family

Q. We want to do right by our family. How should we arrange our IRAs for spouses, children, and grandchildren?

Answer: I assume that you understand tax and creditor advantages of keeping money in IRAs as long as possible. Here's a long-range plan that you might concoct:

1. Say you own a traditional IRA payable to your spouse. At age 70½, you'll take RMDs. At your death, he or she takes control of the account and continues RMDs until death.

2. Then, your spouse passes the account in separate shares to children and grandchildren. Each beneficiary will have a lifeline (life expectancy) that measures their RMDs.

   Example (1): Sandy, a 1-year-old grandchild, inherits a $100,000 share of an IRA. In the following year, her RMD will be merely 1.24 percent of the account. (This is reached by dividing $100,000 by 80.6, your grandchild's remaining life expectancy—as calculated by the IRS. Each succeeding year, the divisor will decrease by one year, becoming 79.6, 78.6, etc.) If the account earns more than its percentage share, it will increase and build over time. This is how to keep an IRA intact for family. Know that if Sandy dies, a new beneficiary assumes distributions based on Sandy's remaining life expectancy.

   Example (2): Let's say Johnny, your 1-year-old grandchild, inherits a $100,000 IRA share with an 81.6 year IRS life expectancy. At age 41, he dies with 40.6 years remaining. Then, his daughter, age 15, inherits the account. Over the next 40.6 years, she'll take RMDs (1 ÷ 39.6, 1 ÷ 38.6, 1 ÷ 37.6, etc.) from the account until it expires. *Note*: If she dies before age 55 (15 plus 40.6), there could even be a new beneficiary to replace her for the remaining years.

A word of caution: These long-range IRA distribution plans embrace an IRA's ongoing tax and creditor protection advantages. And, if a minor will eventually inherit the account, it makes sense to have a trustee or custodian receive and manage his or her RMDs. It's important that everyone understand the objectives. Otherwise, he or she may cash out the IRA early.

Leaving an IRA to a trust

Q. Our family owns IRAs, and many family members and relatives will be direct beneficiaries. Is it better to name trusts as payees?

Answer: What a significant question! This can be a very complex matter. I'll explain.

Presently, at age 70, a traditional IRA owner must take RMDs from the account or pay a 50 percent penalty tax on the shortfall, as I explained in chapter 8 on IRAs.

> *Example (1)*: At age 70½, George, the owner of a $100,000 traditional IRA, begins a series of RMDs. These are roughly equivalent to 4 percent of the account the 1st year and will increase gradually to about 8 percent when he reaches his 87th birthday. (This is based on IRS life expectancies and simple math. It isn't difficult to understand.)

When he dies, George's beneficiary—his wife—can continue RMDs. In fact, she'll get a fresh start. If, for instance, she is age 70½ when George dies, she'll also begin with RMDs of about 4 percent, which will increase gradually to 8 percent when she reaches age 87.

That part is basic. When children, grandchildren, and friends (nonspouse IRA beneficiaries) inherit, things can get complicated. The children must take RMDs immediately, whether the IRA is traditional *or a Roth*. If they don't, there is a 50 percent penalty tax on any required amounts that *should* have been taken.

Example (2): George names his wife as his IRA beneficiary; she designates their children, Scott and Nancy, as primary beneficiaries. She dies when Scott and Nancy are ages 40 and 35, respectively. They receive equal shares of the account and are obligated to take at least small amounts over the next 43 and 48 years (their estimated IRS life expectancies). More precisely, Scott must take at least 1/43, 1/42, 1/41, and so on, from his inherited share. Nancy must take at least 1/48, 1/47, 1/46, and so on.

Unfortunately, Scott and Nancy could get bad advice and cash in their IRA shares. If so, they'll pay taxes too early and lose any ongoing creditor protection. The solution could be a trust-beneficiary that limits their control of the IRA.

Some words of caution: Trusts require record keeping and management. There are tax and accounting fees, tax returns, and taxes at high rates. Generally, it isn't economical (or practical) to divide small IRAs into separate trusts for several beneficiaries. You should discuss this entire matter with a tax and estate planning lawyer before completing or updating beneficiaries on an IRA designated beneficiary form.

A "WHO IS YOUR IRA BENEFICIARY?" DISCUSSION

IRA beneficiary forms are a *very* big deal. They determine who inherits your account and how they are taxed on distributions. Unfortunately, it's easy to lose them, forget to update them, or render them ineffective in other ways.

Since this is so important, let me turn the tables and ask *you* questions:

Q1: *Where is the form?* If it's lost, the remaining questions don't matter much. You'll need new paperwork.

Q2: *Who is the beneficiary listed on the form?* Could he or she now be deceased, disabled, divorced, or a minor who can't legally control an IRA?

Q3: *Are charities, trusts, or an estate listed as beneficiaries?* With the possible exception of some trusts, these entities don't have life expectancies that qualify them as "stretch" payees. Without individuals as designated beneficiaries, the account generally must be cashed in and taxed by December 31 of the 5th year after the IRA owner's death.

Q4: *Who is the contingent beneficiary (or successor after the first beneficiary dies)?* If there is no designee, the IRA is paid to an estate. Then it may have to be cashed out with no more stretch RMDs possible.

Q5: *Do you want to name a successor beneficiary?* Does the form permit this? Or is the decision left to the first beneficiary?

Q6: *Can your beneficiary transfer the account to another IRA provider?* It may not allow this. Is this something you want? If you do, I suggest moving the account to another IRA custodian that will allow a transfer.

Q7: *Is there a minimum account balance?* If so, the IRA may need to be cashed out.

Q8: *Will your IRA provider permit a customized beneficiary designation?* If not, and you can't fit your wishes on the form, you may want to move the account.

Q9: *Does the form assure that the provider will be stretched?*
If you ask them, most IRA custodians and insurance carriers will
tell you that they'll buckle if a beneficiary wants to cash out. If you
want to mandate a stretch IRA, you'll need to assess whether to
move the account.

In summary, IRA beneficiary forms tend to follow the administrative policies of IRA providers—custodians, trustees, and insurance carriers (that provide IRA annuities). Their beneficiary forms
frequently have limits on choices and are confusing to account
owners. That's why you must obtain a new form and bring it to your
financial planner for a review. I can't overemphasize how important
this is.

—

Well, we've now come full circle. In the introduction to *Retirement
Breakthrough,* I *urged* you to create a strong and stable foundation
for your retirement income plan. I recommended these four cornerstones:

- life insurance cash values for withdrawals, policy loans, and
  lifetime incomes;
- annuities, which can pay a lifelong income;
- IRAs/401(k)s and a company pension, where there are mul-
  tiple savings and investment choices; and
- your personal residence.

I explained how these savings instruments—usually in combination (and not individually)—can provide you with a conservative,
secure, and guaranteed rate of return, optimal growth that makes
the best use of current tax law, maximum creditor protection, and
lifelong incomes.

Don't forget, however, that when you introduce these retirement income vehicles to your estate plan, it changes the nature of your estate. Now, wills and trusts no longer control how everything passes to heirs. Large sums of money may pass, instead, via beneficiary forms.

This is precisely why you owe it to yourself and your beneficiaries to familiarize yourself with beneficiary forms and settlement option possibilities. This doesn't mean that wills and trusts are no longer important documents. It just means you've added another dimension to your plan.

As you undertake your planning, speak with other family members. Share your thoughts—and ask for theirs. Families need to talk about money. Parents grounded and secure in their retirement income plan will have less worry and more quality time to help with the grandchildren. Children interested in their parent's financial well-being will feel positive effects well after their benefactor's death.

In short, the whole family is in this together. So please, make time for these critical conversations. Shut the door, turn off the TV, figure out how much money you need for retirement, and make an appointment with your financial planner to talk over the strategies in this book. Then, *implement* the ones that are right for you.

Do this now! Do it while there's still time to maximize your retirement income—and the quality of life in your later years.

AFTERWORD:
HOW WE CAN ALL AVERT A
RETIREMENT INCOME CRISIS

---

*Even though you are on the right track—you will
get run over if you just sit there.*
—*Will Rogers*

I hope you are richly rewarded by reading *Retirement Breakthrough*
and implementing the appropriate planning strategies for you. By
creating lifelong financial security, you not only build the foundation for an excellent life post-retirement, but also eliminate yourself
from the ranks of many senior citizens who will surely live longer
and run out of money. Some pundits predict that a retirement
income crisis, looming on the horizon, will hit us as forcefully as
the stock market crash and housing bust.

I wrote this book to help you avert a personal financial crisis.
But I hope you'll do more than that. I ask you to stand with me in
calling for reforms that will abate this crisis in a holistic, multifac-
eted way—which is the only way to address a crisis of this magnitude, formed by many separate but interconnected issues.

The way I see it, we're all in this together. You may be in a position to address one facet of this multiple-issue crisis, and your neighbor may be in a position to remedy another. But if we all do our part, we can work miracles. Fortunately, we are members of a *participatory* democracy. It is up to *us* to demand that the president, Congress, business and industry, and academia work together on this *now*. If you are in a position to influence decision makers in any of these institutions, I urge you to do so. Please write them a personal note and include a copy of this afterword.

Don't feel you have nothing to contribute. Even e-mails and letters to your Congresspersons and Senators can help move this initiative forward.

Gregory Salsbury, PhD, very cogently dissects the issues in his book *But What if I Live? The American Retirement Income Crisis* (Erlanger, KY: National Underwriter Company, 2006). If you want to understand the retirement crisis in all its dimensions, I highly recommend it. The book is long on analysis, but short on solutions, however. And *solutions* are what I propose.

I want to put the solutions in context, so let me begin by touching briefly on some of the contributing factors:

- First, there is something *very wrong* with a financial system in which the banks are only paying, say, 1 percent interest on savings but charging 15 percent for our credit cards. Americans (the baby boomers especially) have fallen out of the habit of saving money and need extra incentives.

- Second, once upon a time, the working man and woman could count on a company pension. I'll never forget how my uncle relished his "railroad retirement," an income he couldn't outlive. That was in the 1950s. Even as late as the 1970s, there were twice as many traditional "defined benefit" pensions as "defined contribution" profit sharing plans. Now it's the other way around; the burden has shifted to the individual. The system has shifted risk from 401(k)s from employer to employee—yet some 25 percent of eligible employees don't enroll. The 2008 median account balance for those who do is somewhere in the neighborhood of $15,000.

- Third, the graying of the baby boomers means two things: (1) there will be fewer workers paying into the Social Security system to support retirees and (2) the annual cost of social security payments will go way up. Right now, there are about three workers supporting one retiree. That ratio will go down as the 76 to 78 million baby boomers retire. In addition, according to news accounts, Social Security trustees expect—in 2016—to pay out more in benefits than they collect in income. They expect the fund to be totally depleted by 2037—less than three decades from now.

- Fourth, these healthy boomers are going to live longer than their predecessors. At the beginning of the 20th century, life expectancy at birth was merely 47 years. In 2010, life expectancy from birth is 78 years. That's a big leap in one century, considering life expectancy was 36 years from birth for women and 41 to 42 years from birth for men in the Greco-Roman era. Adults over age 80—the fastest growing segment of the population—could have to survive on their retirement income for a good 20 years or more. (Keep in mind that life expectancy is defined as that point—from a starting point—when one-half of that group of people will be dead. Thus, if your life expectancy at age 65 is 85 years old, you have a 50-50 chance of living up to—or beyond—age 85.)

- Fifth, current planning models aren't meant to provide capital for 30 or 40 years in retirement. Take a guess at what will happen if your retirement income plan is modeled on actuarial data that predicts you will die a decade—or three—before you actually do. This is something you absolutely want to avoid.

This is a time for action, however, not despair. Although the train has clearly left the station, I believe there is still time to stop it in its tracks. For starters, let's deal with Social Security before it's too late. Although we know it's being depleted, I predict it will never go under. That's because the government can always raise contributions, reduce benefits, or raise income taxes to keep things afloat.

However, Congress can create "softer landings." I see these next 10 steps as "gentler" solutions than others that have been proposed:

1. Let's increase Social Security's normal retirement age to begin full benefits, reduce cost-of-living increases, and create a quasi partnership between government, the financial services industry, and private business. Encourage the securities industry to create innovative, safe investment alternatives (and let it market them to participants). Then, encourage the insurance industry to give unique payout options such as something for long-term care and an inheritance (and let it market them). The Social Security Administration monitors everything and provides oversight. There could even be public and private options.

2. Expand "Roth IRA conversions" to all tax-deferred money in IRAs, 401(k)s, and employer pensions. Allow this on a voluntary basis and offer an "attractive" flat-tax incentive to make the conversions. Give a 1- or 2-year window to complete things. This will pivot us into a U.S. Retirement Income system that mostly pays out tax free income. Properly promoted, it will also bring in a lot of tax revenue immediately. I really like this idea.

3. Simplify the retirement income market. Keep worker choices, but encourage traditional defined benefit pensions as core programs. Emphasize incomes that can't be outlived. Discourage employee loans and cash outs before retirement. And, in a transient society, encourage benefits portability on the way to retirement.

4. Give full creditor and bankruptcy protection to all funds in Social Security, IRAs, and employer tax-qualified sponsored plans. Shelter this money clearly, whether it is within accounts (or plans), or withdrawn for personal and family support. Assure people that personal funds, dedicated to retirement income, such as IRAs, annuities, and so on, are theirs and can't be obtained by others, no matter who is trying to claim it.

5. Extend the age 70½ date for IRAs and 401(k)s and their RMDs 2 or 3 years out. This extension should build up accounts to last longer in retirement. Condition everything on payouts with life contingencies. Discourage "stretch IRAs" and limit payouts over merely two lifetimes to get money into the economy.

6. Encourage annuities that pay incomes that can't be outlived. Do this by (a) giving annuity incomes a permanent tax exclusion ratio, (b) excluding portions of taxable annuity incomes from taxes, and (c) offering tax incentives to annuitize with a lifetime contingency.

7. To create a strong incentive to build an individual's retirement income capital, allow all taxpayers a sum that they can deduct, grow tax deferred, and receive tax free, as long as it comes from a lifelong income annuity—a fully tax-advantaged account. The alternative seemingly is to tax everyone

so the government can pay out the money and tax it again. The former should be less expensive.

8. Assemble a private panel to make recommendations on Social Security and employer sponsored plans. Ask for a simpler system. Don't use government money to fund this effort or give rooms at an expensive resort as incentives to join this tax force.

9. Educate constituents on how to build and spend a retirement income kitty. Government can only provide so much in Social Security and tax incentives to stimulate personal savings. But it has many public forums through which it can inspire change in Americans' saving and spending habits. Public service announcements could help. Consider this one for starters: "To have $1,000 in monthly income for life beginning at age 65, all you need to do at age 18 is save $65 each month and earn 5 percent interest on it." (Yes, that could be $36,660 paid in—$780 × 47 years, and $480,000 paid to you—$12,000 × 40 years if you reach age 105.)

10. Let's also follow the fine suggestion of the folks at Templeton Press, and reglorify the virtue of thrift by bringing back National Thrift Week (see http://www.bringbackthriftweek.org). I wholeheartedly agree with Templeton's premise that the cultivation of values such as diligence, hard work, responsible consumerism, and smart savings can help "right our floundering economy." Those are the values I was taught in the Iowa farming community where I grew up.

Together, we can make a difference. We've seen what has happened—through the stock market crash and the housing crisis—when we didn't pay heed to the warnings of the experts who prophesied such events. This time, we have a chance to get it right—while there's still time.

ACKNOWLEDGMENTS

This book took 3 years to write. Without the encouragement, assistance, and genuine support of some special individuals, I'd probably have to spend another 3 years to get it done.

I'd like to acknowledge each of them here. I am grateful to:

My son, Scott Duff, who reviewed many drafts, each time offering wonderful suggestions. I am also grateful to his wife, Katherine, who read the manuscript closely and came up with many creative and wonderful ideas.

My good friend and colleague, Tyrone Clark, who insisted that I write this book. I also have Tyrone to thank for dreaming up the great title. Tyrone has remarkable insight on how to improve retirement for all of us.

My dear friend, Caryl Lenahan, who reviewed *Retirement Breakthrough* almost as many times as I rewrote it. Caryl is the type of financial planner anyone would be blessed to have. Her innovative and imaginative views are at the core of this book.

My editor extraordinaire, Deborah Grandinetti, who is at the top of her profession. She is an excellent writer, thinker, and friend—much more than someone who untangles my words and phrases.

My good friend, Gary Mettler, who generously agreed to write the foreword and who also provided many excellent suggestions to improve the chapters on annuities. Gary is the prototype of what a friend should be. When I need a fresh perspective on financial planning, I call Gary. What a resource!

My assistant and bridge partner, Laura Thomson, who surely typed the book manuscript a hundred times. She was always encouraging and insisted I'd get it right if I kept working at it.

My sister, Judy Baur, and her husband, Jack Baur; my friends, Sam Keck, Michael Jangula and Joey Clark; and my bridge partners, Jeff Brown, Forest Clark, Ed Hagerman, Barbara O'Grady, Haisam Osman, Jerry Ranney, and Dan Williams.

Thanks to each of you, more than you can imagine.

APPENDIX A: AN ASSET PROTECTION GUIDE FOR ADVISORS

A: A STATE-BY-STATE LOOK AT HOW THE LAW SAFEGUARDS LIFE INSURANCE CASH VALUES AS WELL AS ANNUITY CASH VALUES AND DEATH PROCEEDS

How much asset protection do the laws in your state provide for money stashed in annuity and life insurance policies—when a claimant is at the ready? I've taken great pains to analyze the law in 50 states, and also in the District of Columbia and Puerto Rico. Realize that the law can change at any time, so be sure to take this chapter to your law library or lawyer and get an update.

The chart that begins on the next page summarizes my results. Let me be very clear that it covers cash values and death proceeds for annuities, but cash values *only* for life insurance policies. That's because there are too many variables to consider regarding life insurance death proceeds to adequately summarize the answers in a chart.

In section B on pages 235–241, I will address insurance death proceeds in depth. I will discuss what you might expect—depending on who the beneficiary is—if a claimant is trying to seize a beneficiary's money. You'll want to pay close attention to this discussion if you're a planner or a beneficiary of a life insurance policy.

This chart can be very helpful if you are comparing the merits of putting serious cash into cash value life insurance versus annuities. As you'll see, virtually all but three states and Puerto Rico provide at least partial safeguarding for personally owned insurance policy cash values. You'll also notice that many states provide greater protection for life insurance cash values than annuity cash values or death proceeds. Minnesota—which provides only partial protection of up to $4,000 for life insurance cash values, but complete (or nearly complete) protection for annuity cash values and death proceeds—is a notable exception.

That said, protection for insurance cash values ranges from full— in states like Alabama, Arizona, Florida, Georgia, New Jersey, New Mexico, New York, Oklahoma, Texas, and Utah (where state laws tend to protect the policy itself and its values)—to no protection in Delaware, New Hampshire, Virginia, and Puerto Rico. In between both poles, states have rules and laws that shelter cash values up to a specified dollar limit (which provides partial protection).

With annuities, shelter from claimants ranges from little (if any) to complete (or nearly complete). As you will see in the chart, Florida provides the greatest shelter for both insurance and annuities, followed by—in alphabetical order—Arizona, Georgia, New Mexico, New York, Oklahoma, and Texas.

State/ Territory	Life Insurance (Cash Values Only)	Annuities (Cash Values & Death Benefits)
Alabama	Full protection	Partial protection for cash values and death proceeds

Alaska	Partial protection up to $12,500	Partial protection for cash values and death proceeds
Arizona	Full protection	Complete or nearly complete protection for cash values and death proceeds
Arkansas	Full protection, as long as the owner is the insured	Little, if any, safeguarding of annuities
California	Partial protection up to $9,700 if single and $19,400 if married	Partial protection for cash values and death proceeds
Colorado	Partial protection up to $50,000	Little, if any, safeguarding of annuities
Connecticut	Partial protection up to $4,000	Little, if any, safeguarding of annuities
Delaware	No protection	Partial protection for cash values and death proceeds
District of Columbia	Full protection if a beneficiary has an insurable interest in the insured's life	Partial protection for cash values and death proceeds
Florida	Full protection	No limitation on exemption of annuity values
Georgia	Full protection	Complete or nearly complete protection for cash values and death proceeds
Hawaii	Full protection if the policy is payable to a "permissible" beneficiary (spouse, children, dependents, etc.)	Complete or nearly complete protection for cash values and death proceeds
Idaho	Full protection, as long as the owner is the insured	Partial protection for cash values and death proceeds
Illinois	Full protection if the policy is payable to a "permissible" beneficiary (spouse, children, dependents, etc.)	Complete or nearly complete protection for cash values and death proceeds

Indiana	Full protection if the policy is payable to a "permissible" beneficiary (spouse, children, dependents, etc.)	Complete or nearly complete protection for cash values and death proceeds
Iowa	Partial protection up to $10,000	Little, if any, safeguarding of annuities
Kansas	Full protection if a beneficiary has an insurable interest in the insured's life	Complete or nearly complete protection for cash values and death proceeds
Kentucky	Full protection, but only in bankruptcy	Partial protection for cash values and death proceeds
Louisiana	Full protection ($35,000 if a policy is issued at least 9 months before attachment)	Complete or nearly complete protection for cash values and death proceeds
Maine	Partial protection up to $4,000	Partial protection for cash values and death proceeds
Maryland	Full protection if the policy is payable to a "permissible" beneficiary (spouse, children, dependents, etc.)	Complete or nearly complete protection for cash values and death proceeds
Massachusetts	Full protection, as long as the owner is the insured	Little, if any, safeguarding of annuities
Michigan	Full protection, as long as the owner is the insured	Complete or nearly complete protection for cash values and death proceeds
Minnesota	Partial protection up to $4,000	Complete or nearly complete protection for cash values and death proceeds
Mississippi	Full protection ($50,000 for values accruing within 12 months of attachment)	Partial protection for cash values and death proceeds
Missouri	Full protection (but only $150,000 in bankruptcy)	Partial protection for cash values and death proceeds

Montana	Partial protection up to $4,000	Little, if any, safeguarding of annuities
Nebraska	Partial protection up to $100,000	Partial protection for cash values and death proceeds
Nevada	Partial protection up to $15,000	Partial protection for cash values and death proceeds
New Hampshire	No protection	Little, if any, safeguarding of annuities
New Jersey	Full protection	Partial protection for cash values and death proceeds
New Mexico	Full protection	Complete or nearly complete protection for cash values and death proceeds
New York	Full protection	Complete or nearly complete protection for cash values and death proceeds
North Carolina	Full protection if the policy is payable to a "permissible" beneficiary (spouse, children, dependents, etc.)	Little, if any, safeguarding of annuities
North Dakota	Partial protection up to $20,000	Partial protection for cash values and death proceeds
Ohio	Full protection, as long as the owner is the insured	Complete or nearly complete protection for cash values and death proceeds
Oklahoma	Full protection	Complete or nearly complete protection for cash values and death proceeds
Oregon	Full protection, as long as the owner is the insured	Partial protection for cash values and death proceeds
Pennsylvania	Full protection if the policy is payable to a "permissible" beneficiary (spouse, children, dependents, etc.)	Complete or nearly complete protection for cash values and death proceeds

Puerto Rico	No protection	Partial shelter for cash values and death proceeds
Rhode Island	Full protection, as long as the owner is the insured	Partial shelter for cash values and death proceeds
South Carolina	Full protection if the policy is payable to a "permissible" beneficiary (spouse, children, dependents, etc.)	Little, if any, safeguarding of annuities
South Dakota	Partial protection up to $20,000	Little, if any, safeguarding of annuities
Tennessee	Full protection if the policy is payable to a "permissible" beneficiary (spouse, children, dependents, etc.)	Complete or nearly complete protection for cash values and death proceeds
Texas	Full protection	Complete or nearly complete protection for cash values and death proceeds
Utah	Full protection	Little, if any, safeguarding of annuities
Vermont	Full protection, as long as the owner is the insured (if the beneficiary designation is irrevocable)	Partial protection for cash values and death proceeds
Virginia	No protection	Little, if any, safeguarding of annuities
Washington	Full protection, as long as the owner is the insured	Partial protection for cash values and death proceeds
West Virginia	Partial protection up to $8,000	Little, if any, safeguarding of annuities
Wisconsin	Partial protection up to $50,000	Little, if any, safeguarding of annuities
Wyoming	Full protection, as long as the owner is the insured	Partial protection for cash values and death proceeds

B. ASSET PROTECTION FOR LIFE INSURANCE: GETTING DOWN TO THE NITTY-GRITTY

In chapter 5, I posed six asset protection questions for you to ask your insurance agent and/or attorney. I said I would answer these questions, based on my own analysis of the law. My answers here are necessarily general, because of variations among the states and the very real possibility that laws may have changed since I wrote this book. Use the guidelines only as talking points for your conversation with your attorney and/or insurance advisor.

Q1: Which state's law applies?

Answer: In any conversation about creditors and the proceeds and avails of life insurance and annuities, it is important to know *which* state's law applies. Naturally, you'd think that it's the state where the policyowner or beneficiary lives. Not necessarily. The state law that applies could be the one in which the policy was taken out or the insurance company is located. Ask your lawyer, "Which law do we use?" And identify whether the situation is in or out of bankruptcy.

Q2: As *policyowner*, are my cash values protected from my personal creditors?

Answer. As I mentioned in section A, virtually all states give at least partial safeguarding for personally owned insurance policy cash values. The results can be surprising. (For instance, in 1996, an Alabama bankruptcy court exempted $2 million of a debtor's insurance cash values.) Sometimes, the outcome depends on who the beneficiary is or whether the beneficiary has an insurable interest in the insured's life.

The protection ranges from none (in states like Delaware and New Hampshire) to full—with many permutations in between, as shown in the chart in section A of this appendix.

Q3a: As a *beneficiary* of a life insurance policy, how am I protected from creditors of (a) the former (now deceased) insured, (b) the policyowner (if other than the insured), (c) myself, or (d) all of us?

Answer: Frankly, the law is not that clear here. When you look at cash values, the pertinent question is whether a mere policyowner is safeguarded from his or her creditors. When you look at death benefits, the possibilities expand. Now the question becomes whether a beneficiary is protected from *anyone's* creditors. These laws really are a challenge. I recommend consulting a lawyer and financial advisor to learn more about the prevailing law that is likely to dictate the outcome in your particular situation.

I will give you my own general analysis, a little further down. (See "Are the Beneficiary's Proceeds Protected from Creditors?" on the next page.)

Q3b: I am a policyowner who wants to ensure that the money goes to my beneficiary rather than anyone's creditors. What do you advise?

Answer: To help safeguard death benefits, it's best to name only individuals or trusts beneficiaries of life insurance. (This is also true for annuities.) Normally, a state will only grant an exemption for death proceeds if the beneficiary is a person or a trust. In most states, proceeds of insurance paid to "my estate" aren't sheltered from anyone's creditors. (However, at least six states—Florida, Iowa, Maine, North Dakota, South Dakota, and Tennessee—have allowed an estate to safely divert the proceeds if payable to protected beneficiaries such as spouse or children.)

There are other reasons not to name estates beneficiaries of insurance money. For instance, the estate will be subject to federal and estate transfer taxes, probate costs, and claims against the estate. This can also increase a surviving spouse's minimum statutory share of a mate's assets—when that could be contrary to the insured's wishes. Here's an example of this increase.

Let's say you own $500,000 in personal assets. According to most state laws; one-half or $250,000 of this will belong to your spouse regardless of what you say in your will. This is referred to as a spouse's "minimum statutory share." You also own a $500,000 life policy payable to your children. If, however, this were paid to "your estate," increasing it to $1 million, $500,000 becomes your spouse's minimum statutory share.

Are the Beneficiary's Proceeds Protected from Creditors?

A breakdown (based on who the beneficiary is)

Here we'll explore the minutiae. (You'll see why this information could not be summarized in the chart in section A.) If you are a beneficiary, a financial planner, or someone with an academic interest in creditor protection for life insurance, you'll want to stay with me through this discussion. Otherwise, you may want to skim this quickly.

Possibility 1: Where I Own a Policy on My Life Payable to You (the Way Life Insurance Is Usually Arranged)

When someone owns a policy on his or her life payable to another party, the states break down protection this way. Either a beneficiary (a) is fully protected from the insured's creditors, (b) is protected only if he or she is a *permissible* beneficiary, or (c) is protected only up to a set dollar amount. In addition, (d) the beneficiary could be protected from his or her own personal creditors.

(a) A beneficiary is fully protected from creditors of an insured who owned the policy.

If I own a policy on my life payable to you, your proceeds are fully protected from my creditors in 34 states, Puerto Rico, and the District of Columbia.

(b) A "permissible" beneficiary—spouse, child, parent, or dependent relative—is protected from creditors of an insured who owned the policy.

If I own a policy payable to you and you are a *permissible* beneficiary, your proceeds are protected from my creditors under laws in 12 states.

(c) A beneficiary is protected from creditors of an insured who owned the policy (up to a set dollar limit).

If I own a policy payable to you, your proceeds are protected from my creditors—up to the state's dollar limit in 4 states.

(d) A beneficiary is protected from his or her own creditors.

If I own a policy payable to you, your proceeds are protected from your creditors in 22 states. These states tend to protect the policy itself and its death benefits. Your next question for advisors is "Are my proceeds protected from my creditors (a) up to and *after* the insured's date of death, or simply (b) up to his or her date of death?" Obviously, (a) is better.

Possibility 2: Where I Own a Policy on Your Life Payable to Me

The usual way a life policy is set up is that I am the owner and insured of a policy payable to my spouse. However, there are situations where I will be owner-beneficiary of a policy on another person's life. For instance, a father/mother cross-own policies on each other or they own policies on children; a business owner owns a policy on another owner or key person; or a creditor-lender purchases insurance on a debtor-borrower.

When someone owns a policy on another's life and also is beneficiary, the states give protection three ways: Either the policyholder (a) is protected from creditors and the insured, (b) is protected from creditors of the insured only, or (c) surprisingly, isn't protected from anyone's creditors. Let's look more closely at each situation:

(a) A policyowner/beneficiary is protected from creditors of both himself/herself and the insured.

If I own a policy on your life and am also beneficiary, my proceeds are protected from both your creditors and mine in 13 states and Puerto Rico.

(b) A policyowner/beneficiary is protected from an insured's creditors only.

If I own a policy on your life and am also a beneficiary, my proceeds are protected from your creditors, but not mine, in 16 states.

(c) A policyowner/beneficiary isn't protected from anyone's creditors.

If I own a policy on your life and am also a beneficiary, some states have strange laws. For instance, my death proceeds aren't protected from anyone's creditors in Alabama, Arizona, Arkansas, Delaware, District of Columbia, Georgia, Idaho, Kentucky, Maine, Massachusetts, Michigan, Montana, New Hampshire, North Carolina, New Jersey, Oregon, Rhode Island, Vermont, Virginia, Washington, West Virginia, and Wyoming.

Whew! That's my analysis of the laws that protect life insurance death benefits that are still sitting in the policy or held by an insurance company.

Q4: What happens when death proceeds (or cash values) leave the insurer and get to someone's checking account? Are these funds protected then and thereafter?

Answer: *Example (1)*: You notify the insurer that you want a $25,000 policy loan. (Can your money be attached as it leaves the policy?)

Example (2): Your father dies and his $100,000 policy payable to you matures; you await a check that is being sent to your checking account. (Will the money be protected from your father's creditors, yours, or both?)

Example (3): Funds in Examples (1) and (2) reach your checking account and are mingled with other money. Or you spend them on luxuries or acquire new investments. (Benefactor: will there be ongoing shelter *after* the funds are in the hands of a beneficiary, which is what you want?)

Now the laws get murky. You'll have the best chance of protecting that insurance money if you:

- live in states like New York or Washington where proceeds have been protected if traceable to an exempt source (the policy itself); or
- keep all payments in a separate bank account; or
- argue that everything is sheltered in Florida, Oklahoma, and Texas where proceeds themselves are protected.

Your account might also be protected in states like Ohio or Tennessee, if it supports your dependents (cash values) or deceased's dependents (death benefits).

In at least Kansas, Missouri, and Ohio, insurance funds reinvested in mutual funds have been turned over to legitimate creditors staking claims. (Even so, I'd keep records that trace the proceeds to the insurer source, and if I did buy that mutual fund, I'd spend its income for support of self and dependents.)

The bottom line: It's prudent to protect a retirement income plan from creditors of self and family. When it comes to shelter for life insurance (and annuities), get straight answers from your lawyer. Make every effort to safeguard the money when it is in the policy, as it leaves the policy, when it gets to your checking account, and/or when it goes into new services, products, or investments.

C. SAFEGUARDS FOR INSURANCE PROCEEDS UNDER SETTLEMENT OPTION AGREEMENTS

I've been referring to so-called proceeds and avails in a life insurance policy. We know that lump sum cash is sometimes protected from creditors of the policyowner (cash values) and policyowner, insured, and/or beneficiary (death benefits). We also know that when cash leaves the policy, protection hinges on a lot of legal language under state laws, as I've just explained.

Observation: There is a way to simplify things. Some 47 states safeguard life insurance (or annuity funds) that remain with insurers under agreements with a "spendthrift clause." The spendthrift clause protects money paid (with interest) in installments over your lifetime or a number of years.

Voila! Creditors are kept at bay. And, in those 47 states, laws or court rulings validate the plan. (Only Idaho, North Carolina, and North Dakota don't seem to recognize these clauses.)

The bottom line: If you or your beneficiary give control of the money to an insurer, you virtually guarantee that creditors are shut out.

Doesn't that sound good in a creditor protection financial plan? Here's what you need to know:

1. When signing forms for a settlement option plan, ask your company to include the spendthrift clause. Otherwise, it might not get put in the paperwork. The people who prepare the forms like to keep things simple. In other words, they'd prefer an agreement without a spendthrift clause.

2. Presently, settlement options are rather stodgy and limited to fixed-lifetime payments, or installments over, say, 20 years. Interest credits may be low. And payments can't be "accelerated" to get at the cash. Personally, I see improvements coming where variable and indexed payouts, cost of living riders, and flexible rights of commutation are added. Beware, however, that a "right to commute" could open up the door for a creditor since you can reobtain control of the money. Again, the "right to commute" essentially means the right to accelerate any remaining payments, converting them once more into a lump sum. (For more information on the right to commute, see chapter 7.)

3. Even though settlement agreements can fortify asset protection, there is an important matter to resolve. Can a creditor garnishee or attach installments once they reach a payee? The answer may come down to whether payments support the policyowner, beneficiary, or his or her dependents; or are clearly traceable back to the insurance company. It may also depend on how fast a creditor gets to the money. Again, everything should depend on state laws, probably where the payee lives.

Q5: If I want to negotiate/arrange a settlement option plan for a beneficiary, should I do this before I die?

Answer: You should! States usually give greater shelter if someone else arranges things.

Q6: If I get into financial trouble, can someone say I paid premiums to defraud creditors?

Answer: About 35 states have specific laws that insurance premiums paid to hinder, delay, or defraud creditors aren't safeguarded from anyone's creditors. Here are some thoughts:

- Assume that all states frown on attempts to hide money from anyone.

- There are numerous noncreditor reasons (including income in retirement) for putting money into cash value life insurance. So a creditor still has to prove that you intended to mislead someone.

- When it comes to premiums under scrutiny, you'll have a chance to show what policy values, if any, are reachable by the creditor. There's no money in a term policy. In cash-value policies, there still may be little, if any, value attributed to paying premiums in question.

D. SAFEGUARDING INSURANCE AND ANNUITIES UNDER A "PERSONAL" CREDITOR PROTECTION PLAN

In Colorado, my home state, it's clear that life insurance cash values are protected from creditors (up to $50,000), but annuity cash values aren't sheltered. (Death proceeds seem to be safeguarded.) However, there is one obscure law on the books that apparently protects *any* money left under settlement option agreements. Seemingly, it assures policyholders and beneficiaries that installments can't be attached when released, received, or reinvested.

In Colorado it seems you might direct cash to an annuity *payout* and never worry over losing to creditors, lawsuits, or bankruptcy. (The arrangement could even include a right of commutation.) If that's so, why not do it? (I mention the Colorado law because you may have a similar law in your state.)

You be the lawyer (or judge)! Here's what the law says:

> **Exclusive right of insured in proceeds:** Whenever, under the terms of any annuity or policy of life insurance, or under any written agreement supplemental thereto, issued by any insurance company, domestic or foreign, lawfully doing business in this state, the proceeds are retained by such company at maturity or otherwise, no person, other than the insured, entitled to any part of such proceeds or any installment of interest due or to become due thereon shall be permitted to commute, anticipate, encumber, alienate, or assign the same, or any part thereof, if such permission is expressly withheld by the terms of such policy or supplemental agreement; and, if such policy or supplemental agreement so provides, no payments of interest or of principal shall be in any way subject to such person's debts, contracts, or engagements nor to any judicial processes to levy upon or attach the same for payment thereof.

And, while it may seem obvious that this law exempts annuity incomes from personal creditors of the payee, a Colorado bankruptcy judge found otherwise in 2007. Is the court right or legislating from the bench? Sometimes you can't tell.

APPENDIX B: RESOURCE DIRECTORY

These are resources, organizations, and individuals that I—or a trusted colleague—personally recommend. This list is not meant to be exhaustive.

Of Interest to Consumers and Financial Advisors

Benefits calculator for social security

If you have enough Social Security credits to qualify for benefits and you'd like to see what's available to you, you will find a Retirement Estimator calculator at www.ssa.gov/planners/calculators. htm. According to information on the site, you can use this for "a retirement estimate based on current law and real time access to your earnings record." It will "provide an estimate of your retirement benefits comparable to the estimate you receive on your Social Security Statement each year, and let you create additional 'what if' retirement scenarios based on current law."

Books by other authors

(Please see the list of my books in the opening pages.)

Dychtwald, Ken, PhD. *Age Power: How the 21st Century Will Be Ruled by the New Old.* Los Angeles, CA: Jeremy Tarcher, 2000. (This book has been lauded as a "wake-up call to debt-laden baby boomers heading toward poverty-stricken old age, to senior citizens, and to society as a whole. Dychtwald, the author of the best selling *Age-Wave*, has written many other excellent books that may also be of interest. I can't recommend his work highly enough. For more information about him, visit http://www.dychtwald.com/.)

Greene, Kelly and Ruffenach, Glenn. *The Wall Street Journal. Complete Retirement Guidebook: How to Plan It, Live It, and Enjoy It.* New York: Three Rivers Press, 2007. (I refer to this book in chapter 1, where I talk about the "one-minute drill" of Charles Farrell.)

Salsbury, Gregory, PhD. *But What If I Live? The American Retirement Income Crisis.* Erlanger, KY: National Underwriter Company, 2006. (Dr. Salsbury deserves kudos for such a cogent analysis of this issue. It has spurred many media reports on the subject.)

Financial education for consumers, companies, and advisors

I highly recommend "**The Allianz: Women, Money & Power Study**" and the tools that were created based on this research. With the help of Ken Dychtwald, Ph.D., president of Age Wave, the Allianz Life Insurance Company of North America set out to quantify the attitudes and behaviors of women and men toward money, finance, and investing. "The Allianz Women, Money, and Power Study," which used Harris Interactive for its survey, examined women in a variety of stages of life and took into consideration varying family dynamics.

For women, it's an enlightening tool that examines what best describes their particular "financial" behavior type: Are you a Financial Dreamer, Financial Avoider, Financial Initiator, Financial

Collaborator, or Financial Analyzer? Knowing this can help you and your financial advisor better understand your decisions and personal approach to planning for your financial future.

For more information about "The Allianz Women, Money, and Power Study," please visit www.allianzlife.com.

Financial advisors, this is also an excellent tool for you. If you understand the five female financial personalities, you can become the ideal financial professional for women, retain their business, and expand yours with financially empowered women.

The Heartland Institute of Financial Education (HIFE), a 501© (3) nonprofit organization, believes that financial well-being is fundamental to the foundation of a successful society. Its mission is to provide quality financial education courses in the workplace or community settings in cities across the nation. Its courses are taught by CFE Certified Financial Educators, and are endorsed by a consortium of colleges and universities.

No solicitation is allowed by instructors, so the courses are offered in a pressure-free, optimal learning environment. HIFE is approved to offer CE credits to HR professionals. The curriculum includes retirement strategies for investing, retirement planning pitfalls, retirement liability issues, and retirement distributions, among other relevant topics.

Go to www.heartlandfinancialeducation.org for more information, or contact Alan Gappinger, CFP, CFEd, chairman and founder of HIFE, toll free at (888) 895-1479.

If your insurance company fails or is on the verge

Contact the **National Organization of Life & Health Insurance Guaranty Associations** (NOLHGA) at 703-481-5206.

NOLHGA is a voluntary association made up of the life and health insurance guaranty associations of all 50 states, the District of Columbia, and Puerto Rico. Since its creation in 1983, NOL-HGA has assisted its member guaranty associations in guarantee-ing more than $21.2 billion in coverage benefits for policyholders and annuitants of insolvent companies. In that time, the associations have provided protection for more than two million policyholders and worked on more than 100 multistate insolvencies. NOLGHA is located at 13873 Park Center Road, Suite 329, Herndon, VA 20171 (E-mail: info@nolhga.com; web site: http://www.nolhga.com).

For information on how to contact the health and life guaranty association in your state, go to: http://www.nolhga.com/contact/main.cfm.

Of Interest to Financial Planners and Advisors

For editorial support

I have relied on **Deborah Grandinetti** for editorial support—for magazine and journal article editing, and book development and editing—for over a decade. If you are planning to write a book, need help editing professional or consumer articles for publication, or want to create materials your clients can understand, I can't recom-mend her services highly enough. She has been a senior editor for a national magazine and a book acquisitions editor for an international trade book publishing company, so she understands what is required to make a magazine article or book publishable and saleable.

You can reach her via e-mail at debgrand@comcast.net or on her cell phone at 215-514-1637.

A professional publicist

Lots of us have a book we'd like to write, but we might lack the time or enthusiasm for the writing process. If so, I help people write their books and book proposals. I also help with almost any kind of publicity. I have a strong background as a writer/editor/PR-media relation professional, and I have a strong journalism background along with direct publishing experience. So, when you're ready to tackle the world of major publishers and New York literary agents, I've been there, done that. I can help you with my experience as an award-winning writer and with a background including *Money Magazine, Life Magazine, Rocky Mountain News, Denver Post, Fortune Magazine, USA Today, NewsWeek, Atlanta Constitution* AND my own successful PR firm. But more about that later, what about you? Do you want to write a book, or book proposal, or launch a publicity campaign? If you do, just shoot me an email or give me a call anytime at 303-692-9774 or smarsh11@msn.com. I'm a long-time friend of Dick Duff and my name is **Steve Marsh**.

For current insurance and financial news

Ranked #1 by Google, InsuranceNewsNet.com (INN) provides 24/7 access to insurance and financial news that matters to advisors and their clients. As a leading content provider, INN uploads more than 150 articles per day on the topics of life insurance, annuities, health insurance, long-term care, disability, and property/casualty. From current legislative headlines to the most compelling retirement research, INN helps insurance professionals and consumers bridge the gap between knowledge and action.

In further support of the educational needs of insurance producers, INN distributes *InsuranceNewsNet Magazine* to well over 50,000 independent agents every month, nationwide. The magazine provides a broad mix of news and sales support articles, including Capitol Hill headlines, sales and marketing ideas, expert insights on running a successful business, interviews with top industry executives, and unique access to the most current marketing research available.

For more information, visit www.insurancenewsnet.com.

For professional education and certification programs:

The Great Life Program from Dr. Linda Ballou can strengthen your transaction and relationship skills in all areas of sales and marketing, and broaden your sales and marketing horizons like top producers. This program is designed to help financial advisors confidently provide educational sessions around four pertinent topics for members of affinity groups, such as credit unions, associations, clubs, churches, charities, hospitals, and schools. The program explains how to align yourself with these groups and walks you through all of the material you would use—such as PowerPoint presentations and presentation material for one-on-one discussions—to present the topics to members of the group.

Dr. Linda Ballou is the creator of the material. She uses it in her own business to generate leads. You can visit her at her website at www.greatlifeeducationalacademy.com.

This educational service will help you expand your client base, retain your employees, and provide better—and more—financial services that are mutually advantageous to you and your clients.

Software to make numbers crunching a breeze

My good friend, Stephan R. Leimberg, CEO of Leimberg and LeClair, Inc., a Bryn Mawr, PA estate and financial planning software company, has created some terrific, time-saving software. Two products I recommend are his **NumberCruncher** software, described as the ultimate "instant answers" solution for estate, business, and financial planners, and his **Financial Analyzer II** software, which puts 75 easy-to-use calculations at your fingertips. *WebCPA* had this to say about both:

NumberCruncher and Financial Analyzer are two more excellent examples of that adage that good things come in small packages. They are simple but effective Windows applications that should have strong appeal for accounting firms engaged in basic analysis and planning. These applications . . . provide an economical and easy-to-use method of handling the widest possible range of basic analytical tasks. They are highly representative of software developed by professionals for their peers in their simplicity, attention to task and precise results.

Just as pertinent for readers of this book is Steve's **Retirement Plan Analyzer 2007.04**, which is designed to evaluate pension and profit-sharing distribution strategies. This tool computes an almost unlimited number of alternatives under methods such as discretionary or attained age. It factors in minimum distribution rules and is updated for the latest tax changes.

For more information about other great products from Steve, go to: http://www.leimberg.com/.

Congratulations on completing *Retirement Breakthrough*! Many people have asked for effective tools that help implement the book's concepts. Go to www.retirementbreakthroughNOW.com for helpful information and services for your next steps. In particular, you MUST answer the **Bonus Questionnaire** for your **Complimentary Personalized Analysis**. It will help you know where you are in relation to the concepts in *Retirement Breakthrough*!

INDEX

O

offshore trusts, 65, 75

P

"Painless Tax Deferment" (Kearns), 163
payout annuities, 134–43, 145–47. See also single premium immediate annuities
pensions, 6–7, 61, 160, 222–23, 225
permanent cash value life insurance, 90–91, 93–95, 100–101
personal income plan. See retirement income goal
personal liability insurance, 65
personal residence. See home ownership
per stirpes designation, 203
Pollan, Stephen, 59
present values (PVs), 20, 97, 151
probate estate, 201–2
public service announcements, 226

Q

qualified plans (QPs)
401(k)s, 6–7, 160, 173–75, 212–13
for asset protection, 68–69, 176–81
and IRA contributions, 169
pensions, 6–7, 61, 160, 222–23, 225
quotients, 45

R

rate of return, 44, 45–47, 101, 103
rating agencies for insurance companies, 85, 100, 119
real estate. See home ownership
required minimum distributions (RMDs)
and 401(k)s, 174, 212
age for starting, 55–56, 158–60, 225
from inherited IRAs, 212–13

penalty for not taking a distribution, 15, 74
and Roth IRAs, 60–61, 160
from traditional IRAs, 159, 161–62
retirement age, 40
Retirement Confidence Survey (RCS), 13
retirement income capital, 6
retirement income goal
amortizing retirement income capital, 19, 34–36
determining how much to save, 30–34, 37
filling in the gap, 37–40
and lifestyle choice, 17–19
overview, 40–42
Social Security factor, 19, 36–37
See also asset protection planning; money growth; tax-advantaged savings programs
reverse mortgages (RMs), 190–92
Reverse Mortgages for Dummies (Lyons and Lucas), 190
reversionary annuities, 108–9
revocable living trusts, 201–2
risk assumptions, 38–40
RMDs. See required minimum distributions
rollovers, 16–17, 212–13
Roth, William, 159
Roth conversions, 170–72, 224
Roth IRAs, 60–61, 158–60, 163–66, 170, 213
Ruffenach, Glenn, 30
Rule of 72, 24–27

S

Salsbury, Gregory, 222
saving money safely, 3–4, 43–45, 84, 87, 218–19. See also asset protection planning; retirement income goal; tax-advantaged savings programs

ABOUT THE AUTHOR

Over a career that has spanned 45 years, Dick Duff, JD, CLU, has provided financial planning counsel to hundreds of individuals across the income spectrum, including some of American's most successful professionals and business owners. He is widely recognized as an expert on how to structure annuities and insurance within an estate plan. He has also gained respect as a teacher of practical financial concepts and solutions for improving personal financial well-being.

Duff is a six-time qualifier for "Top-of-the-Table," the Million Dollar Roundtable's highest award, an insurance industry honor reserved for agents who "provide exemplary client service while displaying the highest standards of ethics and professional knowledge."

In the latter part of his career, Duff has served as an advisor to financial planners and lawyers, who consult him when they need a creative—and legal—solution to a challenging planning problem one of *their* clients has presented. Duff also dispenses advice to financial planners through his online column for *ProducersWEB.com*. He has been a columnist for several professional journals, including *Broker's World*, *CFP's Journal of Financial Planning*, and *Senior Market Adviser*.

Duff is the author of numerous books and manuals, including *Preserving Family Wealth*, *Keep Every Last Dime*, *Take Charge of Your IRA*, and *Money Magic with Annuities*.

Duff is a graduate of the University of Iowa. Semiretired now, he maintains a home and consulting practice in Denver, Colorado. He is the father of two children and the grandfather of two.